Maurice Chevalier

I Remember It Well

MAURICE CHEVALIER

I Remember It Well

PREFACE BY *Marcel Pagnol*
OF THE ACADÉMIE FRANÇAISE

TRANSLATED FROM THE FRENCH
BY *Cornelia Higginson*

THE MACMILLAN COMPANY

Copyright © 1970 by Maurice Chevalier

Copyright © 1970 by The Macmillan Company

All rights reserved. No part of this book may be reproduced or transmitted in any form or by any means, electronic or mechanical, including photocopying, recording or by any information storage and retrieval system, without permission in writing from the Publisher.

The Macmillan Company
866 Third Avenue, New York, N.Y. 10022
Collier-Macmillan Canada Ltd., Toronto, Ontario

Library of Congress Catalog Card Number: 79-126515

First Printing

I Remember It Well was originally published in France in 1969 under the title *Môme à Cheveux Blancs* © Presses de la Cité, 1969.

The title of this book used by permission of Chappell & Co., Inc., publisher of the musical composition "I Remember It Well." All other rights except the title use, reserved by Chappell & Co., Inc.

Printed in the United States of America

To all my American friends.

Having been liked for such a long time in America is the pride of my life.

Maurice Chevalier
4-7-70.

Preface

Here is an amazing book: Maurice Chevalier's own account of his farewell tour and his first months of retirement.

This kind of autobiographical account is very difficult to write. It demands a lot of tact, especially when the narrator's life has consisted of a long string of successes.

Let me say right off that our famous Maurice has found the proper tone without even trying. His book is written freely and without embarrassment, like a letter to a friend.

Granted, he does not have too many harsh words for himself. Sometimes, when he is enumerating his triumphs throughout the world, the reader begins to think that the author is sounding a bit too pleased with himself. But he is wrong. Maurice is very proud of his popularity, but he also finds it a constant source of wonderment. In fact, he is much more surprised than we are at the extent and duration of his prodigious success. He has remained, as he puts it, "an old Paris street kid" still pinching himself to see if what has happened to him is true. He keeps mentioning the encores, the ovations, the full houses, to prove to himself and his readers that he has not been dreaming.

The most remarkable thing about him is that he attributes his success not to his talent but to his hard work, his love for the theater and his respect for his public. We could counter by remarking that we have known plenty of performers who have worked as hard as he, who adored the theater and very sincerely respected their audiences, and never accomplished the half of what he did, simply because they were not born to his beloved mother La Louque.

This account of the last tour of La Louque's son through Europe and the Americas in his eightieth year is a kind of lyric saga that reveals to us his perpetual anxieties.

Will he be able to hold out till the end of his marathon? His shows take place in front of four or five thousand people who have bought their tickets well in advance. A cold, an attack of hoarseness could spell disaster, and that, for Chevalier, means dishonor. The style of his book is wonderfully simple, lively and direct. Its finest moments are those when he explains, with great courage and serenity, how he arrived at his decision to end his career out of respect for his art, his public and his record.

It took him a long time to get used to the idea of retiring. Then he thought of the great popular singer Mayol, who was his mentor and his friend. Over a period of a few years Mayol gave ten or so farewell performances and ended up appearing in a circus between the seal act and the talking mule. He was a pathetic sight.

Maurice was probably thinking of his famous predecessor when he wrote:

> I want the old age of a gentleman artist, philosopher and philanthropist who has come to terms with himself. That is by far the most graceful way to die, but it does not come without self-knowledge. My career will be well in the bag by that time, but I can still tarnish the memory of it, and me, by some parting folly.

I know, I am beginning to talk too much about the problem of my exit . . . but it is the only future I have to discuss. It is so important to me to leave the table before I end up under it!

So now he has retired, and with great elegance, too. But will he be able to stay away from his public? The answer is yes, because he has found a new way to communicate. Before he sang; now he writes. This new book is a worthy successor.

MARCEL PAGNOL

Part One

Eighthieth Birthday Tour

Now that I am pushing eighty, I walk softly and watch where I put my feet. It's a time to be careful. I am stretching my luck to the limit, and a lot of people—including the critics and some of my old fans—are going to object. "Enough's enough," they'll say. "Does he think he can go on forever?"

They don't understand what makes a former Paris street urchin who made it to the top in show business want to break his back to go even higher.

Is it ambition? Vanity?

Neither, I promise you. Maybe it is more like pigheadedness: I am not ready to stop. My success has opened up some new and fascinating vistas to me, and I want some more time to explore them.

And then there is the question of my public. Except for my mother, nothing in my life has meant more to me. I have lived and breathed for my public, and in exchange it has lifted me to where I am today.

Don't worry, I am not going to get sentimental. I won't get down on my knees and sing you a hymn of thanks, or bombard you with memories, or anything like that. I just want you to know that as long as there are a few of you left who believe in my sincerity and a few of you who are happier when you hear me sing, I will keep on singing and trying to improve. And, despite all my failings, I don't intend to stop until I figure that I am no longer a credit to the memory of *la mère Chevalier* or the profession that adopted me as a child and gave me its backing.

Life in today's world is a kind of sport. And can you think of any better way to play it than to be in the game to win?

Performers have two different ways of looking at their audiences. Some think, well, they paid to see me and I did my best. So why should I be grateful for their applause? I earned it.

The others, including me, feel eternally grateful to this friend of many faces. Without our public, we would never have mustered up the confidence and courage we needed to go on. It did not take me long to realize, when I was starting out, that you have to have a public to be an entertainer. As long as the public wants you, you're on; when the public loses interest and seeks amusement elsewhere, you've had it. You're washed up.

But if the public feels you are sincere, and of course if you have talent, you have a lifelong friendship that can be more solid than the best of marriages. So that is why I always tell young hopefuls, "Love the public the way you love your mother. Your mother gave you life; your public can help you live life to the fullest."

I just took Laurent, son of my cook Maria, to see the Moscow Circus at the old Cirque d'Hiver in Paris. What a magnificent show! The acts have improved immensely; a couple of years ago, the opening number would have been the grand finale. The jugglers, acrobats, balancing acts, all of them perform feats that make earlier ones look commonplace. I am an old circus buff, and I could hardly believe my eyes.

Why be so surprised? After all, unbeatable records get beaten all the time in the world of sports. The show ended with a wonderful bear act. Big ones and little ones balanced on bicycles and motorcycles and did tricks that most of us could not do. As soon as they had accomplished their tasks, the shaggy things came over to collect their sugar lumps as meekly as little pups.

During the performance I glanced up from time to time at the balconies where I used to sit with my mother and brothers of a Sunday evening—just before the turn of the century. Seats cost next to nothing in those days; I was ten years old and already bitten by the bug. My life's ambition was to be an acrobat like Fratellini, and Francesco, the equestrian performer, and the boys who did flips in the air.

The minute the circus was over, Laurent asked to sit through the second matinee performance. When I said no, he consoled himself by jumping up onto all the benches lining the Boulevard des Filles de Calvaire to prove that the children we had just seen performing had nothing on him.

One day the singer Marcel Amont invited me to lunch in the country house where he lives with his father and his mother, a handsome woman of the people, and the love of his life, a rare pearl, one of the singing and dancing Kessler sisters. Our conversation turned to the *chansonnier* George Brassens, whom Marcel knows intimately and who has just recovered from a serious operation. We expressed the hope that his recent Académie Française prize for poetry had been some consolation to him. I had known Brassens when he was starting his singing and songwriting career and had given him a lot of encouragement, but I had never invited him to lunch at my house because I knew he shunned society. At my request, Marcel brought us together.

For the time being George Brassens dominates the music-hall world by the sheer strength of his personality. He comes on exactly as he is, his handsome face radiating modesty, good will and compassion. Sometimes you have the feeling that his own openness embarrasses him. In any event, his talent has so much freshness and poetry to it that he has a right to behave the way he wants. His awkwardness is in character; he wouldn't be so likeable if he were relaxed and smooth. In a sense, he is not even performing; he is singing about what is on his mind in a fine masculine voice. Like many of the great *chansonniers* of the past, he writes his own songs, and many of them are haunting.

Brassens sees practically nobody besides his audiences and an intimate circle of friends. He turns down all invitations and refuses to alter his way of life. Is he right or wrong? My opinion is that a performer cannot keep entirely to himself; he needs to get out and see other performers and be inspired by what they do. Brassens does not seem to agree. He almost never goes to the theater or recitals, or even to the movies. He reads and thinks a lot and writes when he feels like it. Conversation with people he doesn't know is painful for him.

I wonder though. Perhaps I am mistaken, but I got the impression that Brassens is beginning to suffer from his self-imposed solitary confinement and to realize that he needs other people to develop as a performer and a person. Naturally, we did not talk about it. Brassens is the kind of person you want to help, but can't, because he is far too proud and secretive to tell you about his inner doubts and fears.

For the past six days we have been in Montreal. Tomorrow I make the first of twenty-odd appearances in a stadium seating 25,000 people. Of course I won't be alone all evening; 500 other entertainers will perform before and after me in the three rings of the Expo Autostade. When my turn comes, the three rings will empty. Brief scenes from my biggest movies will be flashed onto giant screens, followed by a brief introduction filmed by Jean-Christophe Averty. Then I will sweep around the stadium in an open car like Nero in a boater and disembark at the foot of a twelve-foot-high platform that I am to mount majestically. There, under enormous spotlights and all alone except for my accompanist, Fred Freed, I will have the job of recreating the intimate atmosphere I am famous for.

You can imagine my reaction when I first saw the stadium. *What? They want me to sing in here? They are out of their minds!* I could throw myself into my performance with everything I had and I would still look like a gesticulating ant. What they were asking me to do amounted to professional suicide.

I couldn't sleep. I was scared out of my mind. And the next morning I had to help the publicity people, give interviews and a press conference and show up at Expo '67, which did indeed look like a triumph for the city of Montreal.

The press conference lasted an hour. Even when they were bombarding me with questions I could sense the sympathy that these journalists had for France and Frenchmen, and I began to regain my confidence. The crowds helped too. While I was being shown around the Canadian pavilion in the company of two imposing but affable policemen, people cheered me and called out my name: "Long live Maurice Chevalier," "*Vive la France,*" "*Bonjour, Momo*" (one of my oldest nicknames). I felt better by the minute.

A charming guide showed us through the French pavilion from bottom to top. Our offering at Expo was in tune with the high quality of the rest. That further reassured me.

I certainly slept like a log that night! And when I woke up the following morning, I couldn't remember where I was, and it took me several minutes to recall that I had come to Expo '67 in Montreal to sing intimate songs to 25,000 people a night. Now that I was more rested, the task did not seem so impossible. No, this was not an ordinary engagement, but what had I expected at a World's Fair?

I had been sent to represent my country and I had to prove that I was worthy of the honor. For some reason or other I started to think of Sarah Bernhardt's American tours—the Barnum and Bailey-like fanfare, the parades, the crowds of well-wishers. If the organizers of Expo had decided on me rather than on some younger French star, it was because I was more than an elderly singer: I was the French flag personified. So be it. Sarah and her legendary courage would lead me into battle. I thought of General de Gaulle's worldwide trips. He had gone to Mexico and South America, scarcely recovered from an operation, to speak to the people in their own language: "*la mano en la mano. . . .*" This is not a political judgment; I shun politics like the plague. But the thought of him was fortifying. Suddenly I felt that Sarah and *le grand Charles* were beside me. Then I remembered some words that Prince Charles of Belgium, Count of Flanders, had said to me over lunch at my house about "divine intervention," and lo and behold, a third figure joined me. No longer would I have to face that monumental crowd alone. Three other people would be up on that platform with me to whisper, "Take heart, Momo," every time I faltered. Aside from this brief moment of pluck, I spent the rest of the time before opening night in the grips of the worst stage fright imaginable.

The dreadful evening arrived. An enormous crowd filled the stadium. Everything went well until the Gemini were halfway through their trapeze act, suspended from a helicopter. Then a fine rain began to fall. I had just the time to say to myself, "Only a summer shower," when it started to pour. I forgot to say this was an open-air stadium.

It poured. The show was stopped and people began to scurry around like ants, seeking shelter. Just when the management decided we would sit it out, the deluge started. Catastrophe. I was sitting in my dressing room trying to preserve whatever self-control I had and determined to let nothing faze me. I must have looked like one of those dogged old soldiers who have seen so much that they don't care if they live or die. Whereupon the show was called off and everybody got his money back.

That's the breaks!

July 13, 1967. Last night was the second attempt to open the show. Just before it was to begin, another storm broke over Montreal. Did it mean a second false start? The management would let us know in half an hour.

The downpour stopped as abruptly as it had begun, and the show started only thirty minutes late. Everything went like clockwork and the crowd seemed pleased. My turn came. I made my triumphal entry to the applause of the multitudes that seemed to find nothing unusual in these heroics. As soon as I mounted the platform, I realized that I couldn't see my audience any better than they could see me, because I was blinded by the spotlights. But I seemed to be communicating. They were laughing in the right places. They clapped when they were supposed to. Whew! I was going to make it.

My third song was preceded by a little introductory speech. No sooner had I embarked on it than an infernal racket started up behind me and got louder and louder till I had to stop. I couldn't even hear the sound of my own voice. Shouting into the microphone, I asked the management to do something, and a voice over a loud-speaker assured me that the necessary steps had been taken. I waited. The sound got weaker, then started up again. I kept myself and my audience in hand with a continuous patter. The noise—due, it seemed, to the maneuvers of a train in an adjacent station—had been going on for fifteen minutes when the audience began to shout at me to get back to singing.

So I did.

Needless to say, I had to yell out my songs, and not much was left of the old Chevalier touch. But the results were gratifying. This morning Montreal's biggest English newspaper devoted a marvelous article to me. I read it groggily—and proudly—after my bad night's sleep. From now on, I've decided, I will have to be prepared for anything to happen. After all, it is not every year that there is an Expo '67, and it is not every year that I set out on an Eighthieth Birthday Tour! This is a Big First and a Big Last, and I will have to rise to the occasion.

I had less trouble last night during my second performance. There were no cataclysmic interruptions, only a jet flying directly overhead at two different intervals. This time I was unruffled and went right on singing. The jet was music to my ears compared to the engine that played accompaniment to my first performance. And besides, this time I was confident that I could communicate with 25,000 people and still stay within the limits of the Chevalier style. I have been telling myself that this stint will be just one more adventure to chalk up to experience —provided I survive all the performances to come.

Meanwhile I will have the opportunity to devote each afternoon to a different pavilion at the fair. What a fine way to pass the time! It won't take me long to recover from the first two performances, and since it has always been my rule to recover from the worst in the best and most long-term way possible, I will stick to my tradition and forge ahead.

Expo '67 is a show that revealed a great new star—the city of Montreal. And Canada has profited from the occasion to emerge in the eyes of the world as a young and determined country looking resolutely to the future. We have already seen the handsome big display at the Canadian pavilion. The breathtaking film shown inside was supervised, up to the time of his death, by the great Walt Disney. It covers three walls like a giant Cinerama. While you are watching it you feel as if you are seeing all seven wonders of the world at once. The English pavilion features a series of "flashes" projected one after another onto niches in the walls. They illustrate episodes from English history from the beginning to the present, with its maxi-hair, mini-skirts, Carnaby Street and the Beatles. It was an enchanting creation.

There are more films at the American pavilion, this time projected onto five screens arranged in a pyramid.

The subject is children of all walks of life and colors playing their favorite games. The children were adorable, the photography magnificent. Another display told the story of Hollywood, with giant portraits of its stars. And then there were satellites and space capsules retrieved from the sea after re-entry, and a replica of the module that should soon be making a moon landing.

Yesterday we saw the Labyrinth, a specially constructed room where you remain standing so that you can look up and down, in front and behind you at the enormous screens on all sides. Across these screens pass pictures of the earth, the sky, the city, the countryside; the birth of a child, his progress through adulthood to old age, and his struggle to come to terms with himself. What a spectacle! I was fascinated from beginning to end.

Nothing at Expo is more exciting than this revelation of what is happening in the field of cinematography. The movies we see in traditional theaters are old-hat by comparison. When Jean-Christophe Averty arrived in Montreal to make the introductory film for my show, he was amazed and inspired by these revolutionary works. I think everybody involved in filming for the movies or television owes it to his art to subject himself to the same experience.

The kinks in my show are ironed out. I get the feeling that I have succeeded in creating a certain intimacy between me and my almost invisible audience. The miracle takes place thanks to the technical perfection of the acoustical arrangements and also because of the warmth and generosity of these international audiences. Thank goodness!

But this success does not excuse the original error in judgment on the part of the producers. Our show is bright, modern and full of talented people, but it will never be perfect. It just isn't possible really to reach an audience seated in a sports arena.

It was especially a mistake to put me in there. I have always relied on nuances in my voice and facial expressions to get my points across, and obviously they get lost in an enormous stadium. I have managed to survive, but look at the odds against me! The size of the Expo Autostade. The planes and trains buzzing by. Not to mention the problem of Canadian bilingualism: I am forced to mix English and French without offending the very sensitive French Canadians. Perhaps you are beginning to get an idea of what I go through each night.

And yet—the size of the challenge makes me even prouder of my victory. This may well be the most satisfying success of my long career. According to my contract, I am supposed to stay on that platform for no more than twenty-five or thirty minutes, but encores keep me up there for twenty minutes more. By the time I reach my dressing room I am as pooped as I usually am after a two-hour performance.

Two weeks left to go. I intend to survive them.

The show goes better every night, despite my reservations. Something has clicked, after our difficult debut.

Good showmanship can always triumph over adversity! Meanwhile I am trying to behave myself and do nothing to jeopardize the success of what is to come. After all, my reputation is at stake. I am more relaxed. The audience is more responsive. This is not the time to falter.

Halfway through. I can finally see the end of this Expo engagement that has strained my head, heart and stomach.

Taking stock, I feel I have really made the Big Time. Each night we take in more customers. Each night we have a crowd big enough to fill ten ordinary theaters. And thanks to the well-placed microphones and speakers, I'm getting to them, I'm making that old intimate contact. This show of Leonidoff's is the biggest, the most modern and spectacular extravaganza that I have ever starred in. What's more, I am getting the biggest fee of my career. Too bad I didn't know before I was up to this kind of production. Now it's too late to make it my specialty.

Yesterday afternoon we were taken through the Soviet pavilion by two officials, one our guide, the other a friendly character who just came along with us. The displays showing the scientific, industrial and artistic accomplishments of the Soviet Union left me openmouthed with astonishment. Old Russia has been replaced by a new one, vigorous and wholesome. At the end of our tour, we were ushered into a little projection room where piped-in Russian folk songs filled the darkness. Then the show began. We were supposed to be inside a capsule, hurtling toward the moon; clouds parted and we were in the realm of the stars; the sky twirled around as if we were making loop-the-loops. I really did feel as if I were an astronaut penetrating the unknown. Finally we descended over Moscow, which looked very impressive under its blanket of snow. The film ended with some peaceful sentiments that nobody would contest, if peace would make it possible for everybody to duplicate the accomplishments we have seen at Expo. And make us lead more reasonable lives as well.

The miracle continues. We are into the second half and the box-office sales keep mounting. My vocal cords, usually so capricious, seem to be thriving on a diet of wind and noise served under an open sky. The only challenge they have yet to meet is singing in the rain, protected from the elements by nothing but a boater. Every day I spend an hour practicing with my accompanist Fred Freed. If my health holds out, I think the best recital of my career is yet to come. That is what I live for. I learned to be good ages ago, so now all that is left to me is to polish my performances. The rest of the time I can sit back and enjoy the inner peace and contentment that being reasonable has brought to your friend Saint Momo. Soon enough I will have the time to devote myself to being truly serene and philosophical. After all, I can't say that the story of my life has had a happy ending if I haven't learned to come to terms with myself and with my old age.

Tomorrow is our last night at the stadium. My next engagement is in Flint, Michigan, and we have just heard that the show will go on despite recent racial troubles. That would be the last straw, to have to go on singing placidly while people were fighting in the audience! Luckily, Montreal has trained me always to be ready for the worst. Yesterday while I was singing, not only did the train go by making its usual racket, but also a helicopter and a plane. They hovered so long over the stadium that I thought some overaffectionate fans had decided to view me from a new and original angle.

Yup, I have learned not to frazzle easily. My twenty evening performances have prepared me for the future. Everything from now on is going to seem like a bed of roses—another reason why this experience has been worth it.

July 30, 1967. The ordeal is over. Twenty nights and three matinees later, I think I can say I passed muster in a situation demanding more gall than talent. My success makes me all the prouder because I was working under such tension, although I got a lot of help from my charming audiences. Another reward, of course, was being able to visit all the pavilions devoted to human advancement. In addition, I am leaving Montreal in fine voice. Being made to sing outside over the noise of wind, Expo, trains and planes seems to have given it a new lease on life. I am relieved that my future engagements are less "Barnumesque." But I would not have missed this one for anything; I am the richer for it.

We are in Flint, Michigan, near Detroit, where I have performed despite recent racial troubles in the black sections of the city. The place is so calm and friendly that it is hard to believe that violence and murder are lurking beneath its calm exterior. The superb hall where I sang last night was filled to cracking with a very dressy audience. The program that I did for them will serve as the basis for my Eightieth Birthday Tour, starting in October. My new routines have fulfilled all my fondest hopes. Now I need to work with them a bit so that I can use them with more finesse. Whenever I am trying out new material, I am not too subtle. I want my stuff to get across. Then, when the songs and routines have proven themselves, I let up the tension because I am sure they will work.

Last night, two hours of working with an old microphone and new material really tired me out. Next we go to a theater tent in Hyannisport, where I hope to recover and polish things up.

I have decided that my goal is to go on for another year or so and then stop all tours and recitals. It is now August, 1967, and a lot of my one-man shows will cross the boards before I'm through. I think I can realize this beautiful dream, but it is not a time to be overconfident. First of all, there is the question of my health, my nerves, my determination to go on. And then, who knows what will happen to the U.S.A. in the next few years if it does not find a way out of its terrible dilemmas? But that's not my problem—not much I can do about it. I have an engagement in Hyannisport to do. And there is a chance I may see Jacqueline Kennedy, who is vacationing there with her family-in-law; I admit that a rendezvous with her would be the highlight of my trip and a reward for my monastic life as missionary of the entertainment world.

Hyannisport, August, 1967. There is only one word for the weather in this famous resort—terrible—and they say it has been that way since the beginning of the summer. The rain has emptied the hotels and motels, and their owners are gasping like fish stranded on the beach. As a result, there were fewer people than expected at my opening under the Melody Tent last night, but their warmth and enthusiasm more than made up for their lack of numbers. That is why I will take the theater any day over any other medium. There is usually something forced about a television or radio or screen performance, but the live contact with a live audience is always absolutely real.

As I had hoped, these appearances are giving me a chance to perfect my Anglo-French recital before the supreme test of this fall's Eightieth Birthday Tour. The material is shaping up, and the addition of new songs and ideas has given my show a real lift. I prefer these theaters-in-the-round to ordinary theaters; they facilitate contact with the audience. I finish each show feeling stronger than when I started, and a little strength is all Papa Momo needs to finish up his business.

The weather continues to be awful. It rains, it blows, the barometer leaps up and down in a sadistic fashion. Last night we were shivering—in the middle of August!

But what difference does the weather make when you like your work and the way you run your life? Let it rain. The sun is shining inside you. Especially when you arrive in Hyannisport to find a note from Jacqueline Kennedy waiting for you. What was my pleasure? she asked. Lunch, a boat ride, a swim, whatever my heart desired during my stay in Hyannisport, she would provide it. I am not strong on sports while working, but the idea of lunching with Jackie was just what the doctor ordered. By telephone we decided that I should come to the compound on my very first day, and that is how I met nine-year-old Caroline, already lovely, and her handsome little brother John-John. These two famous children were as intimidated by me, a strange old gentleman, as I was by them. Their mother insisted on driving me back to my hotel herself, and then and there we set the hour for lunch the next day at the house of friends, Mr. and Mrs. Paul Mellon. Jackie, adorable as always, came to fetch me in her car and drove me back after lunch, chatting about this and that.

There's more. She came to see an evening performance at the Melody Tent with her sister-in-law, Ethel Kennedy. They crept into the back row to avoid being noticed and then came backstage afterward to see me in my dressing room. Jackie looked as radiant as a happy child. The time I spent with her put me in fine spirits for the remainder of my week in Hyannisport. My work was going well, too. All in all I was glad to be an old troubadour who still had the capacity to marvel at his own good fortune.

The second happy surprise of my stay in Hyannisport was a book: Cornelia Otis Skinner's *Madame Sarah,* about Sarah Bernhardt. I liked it so much that I immediately wrote to the author asking her to send me a book label with a word or two of dedication that I could paste in my copy. Of course I knew that Cornelia Otis Skinner was a great American actress and a specialist in the "one-woman show." I also remembered that she was very attractive, a woman of our world, in sum. But I had no idea that she was a writer, too. This revelation made me move her to the top of my list of show-business "greats." The letter she sent me in return gave me the impression that Cornelia Otis Skinner and I were fated to be friends. We have just given each other the same kind of encouragement, because, being performers, we are both especially appreciative of admiration returned in kind! I am eager to meet her and hope she will lunch with me at my house the next time she comes to Europe. I have not aged like other people, and neither has she. We keep forging ahead, doing new things and meeting new people, and that way we avoid the depressions that so often hit oldsters who can't admit that bygones are bygones.

In a few minutes I set off for another theater tent near Boston where I will make four appearances. After three more shows in still another tent nearby, we fly from Boston to Orly and home. Home is my house in Marnes-la-Coquette, outside of Paris, that I have named after my mother: La Louque, the nonsensical nickname my brother and I gave her when we were little.

Hurray! I can hardly wait.

There are two sides to my character. The first is active, eager and excitable. The other is modest, timid and cautious, and that is the one that has enabled me to get this far without any terrible disasters and the one I am counting on to see me to a dignified end.

I'm too old for the temptations that led me around by the nose when I was younger. I can't go down the primrose path at my age; it leads to disaster, via shame and despair, and don't think I don't know it. I am not an unpopular old man, and people still make me all sorts of exciting propositions, but I have learned to resist because I have no desire to go "the way of all flesh." All I want is to fulfill my own destiny and earn the right to be at peace. That may mean some hard decisions, but they will not be the first: the good image that people have of me has been my reward for sticking to decisions that were more a matter of common sense than anything else. Now at the time of reckoning I am reaping the fruits of my good behavior. Serenity. Contentment.

Beverly, Massachusetts: Another theater-in-the-round, the prettiest so far. It attracts people from all over New England, and I have enjoyed their company. My relationship with the critics has been harmonious, too; the dean of Boston critics, Mr. Elliott Norton, came to interview me for television yesterday. My two hours under the bright lights practically finished me, and I have concluded that I must be kinder to myself during the day. This is, if I want to make it to my eightieth birthday next year and celebrate it as planned. If only I don't start getting the anxiety attacks that have dogged me ever since my nervous breakdown forty-five years ago.

Last night was my final performance in Beverly, and it was so successful that I could not sleep from an overdose of happiness. This morning's *Boston Herald Traveler* contains an article called "The Greatness of Chevalier." We are about to leave for Cohasset, Massachusetts, not far away.

When I got home to Marnes-la-Coquette, I found an invitation waiting for me. My friends Marta and Lucien Barrière were suggesting that I come to spend five days with them at the seaside resort of Deauville. Off again! But this time to relax.

Félix and Maryse Paquet, my companions at La Louque, came along to share the bracing air and bubbling talk the Barrières always offer. We started out during lunchtime in the hopes that there would be less traffic. At Evreux we came upon a road accident. These new superhighways get you places faster, but they also make for more serious accidents. We arrived in Deauville late and with our throats tight and dry.

While Maryse was setting us up at the hotel, I took a stroll around the Casino to window-shop and put myself into the Deauville mood. Later Marta Barrière joined me, looking very "mod" on the outside but on the inside just the same wise and unaffected woman as ever. We strolled down the boardwalk under the partly cloudy sky and then stopped for a peppermint frappe at the Bar du Soleil.

No, Deauville is not what it used to be. The people are no longer so elegant. The general tone has become—well, more middle class.

After a brief nap we went to dinner at the Ambassadeurs, a restaurant with a floor show inside the Casino. There was nobody there worth mentioning, just some oldish café-society types without much sex appeal! You can tell they represented Big Money. It was written all over them, though they tried to look a lot more dignified than they really were. Basically they were outgoing and friendly. Did the constant effort give them cramps? I wondered. They danced in the traditional manner; none of them seemed to have heard of the frug. Well, there was nothing aggressive about them, and they did have a certain white-haired elegance.

Meanwhile we ate a splendid dinner. It was hard to keep from stuffing ourselves on the succulent dishes our host kept serving. We washed down the feast with a fine champagne that tasted like nectar, and soon I began to realize how much I had needed to play hooky after my strenuous stint in the United States. When dinner was over we watched our friends Suzy Volterra and Tonia Derval nonchalantly playing baccarat for what looked like very high stakes.

Then I began to ask myself: Do I still find this kind of life amusing? Was it worth my while to come? After a good night's sleep, a breakfast of good *café au lait,* a stroll down the boardwalk and lunch at the Bar du Soleil looking at the crowds, I was sure that the answer was—yes. Why not be just another vacationer letting himself go for his few days of freedom a year?

And there were lots of things to do—crowds on the beach to watch, grandmothers sitting in the bosom of their families, shapely women and tanned children stripped to the bare minimum. There were past acquaintances who came up to me eager to talk about old times. There was even an invitation to cocktails from the lady mayor of Deauville, Madame d'Ornano. I was caught up in the rhythm of a charming young existence that had the kindness to adjust its pace to include an old boy like me.

What is more, the old boy was looked at, photographed, accosted. He got living proof of what he still means to all generations in France.

Far be it from me to be ungrateful for their homage. I like to be liked. All my life I have worked to attain that magnificent state of grace. Why else would I still be exercising my profession as salesman of sunshine and love?

They say that all or almost all women's-clothes designers these days are homosexuals who in their heart of hearts cannot stand women. You believe it when you see them turn young females into boyish apparitions that must correspond somehow to the young men of their dreams. Last night we attended a Patou showing. The models were so bereft of what makes women women that you wondered if they had not all been planed down in a sawmill to look like Twiggy. Even their masklike faces seemed sad and undernourished. If this is fashion, Marilyn Monroe restored to us would never make the grade.

Brigitte Bardot and her millionaire playboy are staying at the Royal Hotel and studiously avoiding everybody and everything that does not interest them. The general public is not reciprocating; it watches their passage with breathless fascination. I saw them the other night playing roulette at the Casino. He stood next to her tossing around chips worth a million old francs as if they were pennies.

Actually, I am an old admirer of Brigitte's and have been for the fifteen years since she came to my house to play a model in a television sequence I was filming with the painter Van Dongen. After that she skyrocketed to fame, and I never saw her again. Reichenbach, the film-maker, has asked me to do a program with Brigitte for American television, and I have been wondering if our two personalities would mesh. I have a feeling they wouldn't. This has happened before. In the past I have admired people like Sacha Guitry and Henri Bernstein but did not want to appear in their plays because I felt they weren't my style. When I get back to Paris, Reichenbach is supposed to tell me what he wants me to do with the little princess. I think I will follow my instincts.

Ah, I just saw her go by on the boardwalk, with her small band of friends. What a splendid apparition! A hint of self-consciousness in her walk, eyes skyward as if she were attacking the future, she looked distant, beautiful and more than a little bit petulant.

We are back in Paris after spending five restful days in Deauville at the height of the season. The holiday was a welcome diversion from my life of work and recitals. Now that life begins again. The Eightieth Birthday Tour is approaching, with all that entails from the point of view of responsibilities and risks. No matter what happens from now on, I shall stick to the beaten track. In my case, that means being modest, amiable and mindful of the fact that I owe everything to a faithful lucky star.

Since my seventieth birthday, I have looked on each new morning as a personal gift from heaven.

The first leg of my Eightieth Birthday Tour has officially started.

We—my assistants François and Madeleine Vals, my accompanist Fred Freed and I—left Orly Airport this morning in a great flurry of newsmen, television cameramen and photographers (fourteen, I counted). I was reminded of my spectacular departure for Hollywood forty years ago. Air France had provided an enormous cake in the form of a boater. Mireille Mathieu, the younger generation's adorable answer to Edith Piaf, was leaving that day for Munich and came over to help me cut it. Cake and champagne provided a proper send-off for my last international tour.

All the same, my heart was pounding. I felt like an automobile racer who knows that his rage to win may drive him into oblivion. Like him, I was leaning too hard on the accelerator. Suddenly it was very difficult to tear myself away from my La Louque household, the people who are so much a part of my daily life and whom I try so hard to do well by. My companions Maryse and Félix Paquet drove me to Orly, and I had a lump in my throat when the time came to say *au revoir*.

Here I am in Kansas City after a long and tiring trip. I have exactly two days to pull myself together and adjust to the time change before I enter stage left. It's back to work again.

I did not even dare ask if the tickets had been selling well, because I was not sure I wanted to know. I feel like the typical weary stranger in the big city. Already I am tired at the very thought of asking more of my rusty old motor. We are staying in one of those Holiday Inns you find all over America. It is an egalitarian, utilitarian and comfortable place. Every guest gets the same windowless room, the same push buttons for operating lights, heat, air, radio and television. The service is prompt and the food fresh and well prepared. The prices are not too bad, either. Here is one tired traveler who really appreciates American democracy's contribution to tourism.

After a light sleep and a light breakfast, I remembered. I am in Kansas City, Missouri, where my job will be to make some Americans love a Frenchman, despite the deteriorating relations between our two countries.

Think how boring life would be if we had no problems!

So much of my life has been spent working and traveling that I have never had enough time to read. Now I am making up for lost time. In my eightieth year I have discovered Simone de Beauvoir and feel as if I have struck a rich vein of moral support just when I need it most. I read her page by page, pausing to digest thoughts that touch me more than anything I have ever read by another woman writer. Every page is filled with a love for life and a wonderful sense of words. She is opening up new vistas for me.

Life is really strange. I would never have discovered Simone de Beauvoir if my nineteen-year-old great-niece Mimi Chevalier had not handed me *Memoirs of a Dutiful Daughter*, saying that the author mentioned me a couple of times in her extraordinary book.

I am not sure that Simone de Beauvoir, who is reputed to be very antisocial, would want to waste her time getting to know someone like me. I am determined to meet her, anyway, perhaps through the intermediary of Jean-Paul Sartre, who once said he was an admirer of mine. I know already what I would tell her: how much I appreciate her talent as a writer and how grateful I am for the moral support I have derived from her books.

No, I am not completely rested yet. But tonight I perform in a splendid theater completely sold out, and I have to win their hearts. There is more to my fatigue than the trip alone; yesterday I had to survive a gala reception that I should have been spared.

My hosts were the members of the Alliance Française of Kansas City, a group with several hundred members, and they held their reception in a fancy new store. I had promised to drop by, thinking that all that was expected of me was a little speech. But no, I was to be introduced to each member, one by one. A line formed and I stood at the head of it like a visiting chief of state shaking hands and replying to the kind words that these gracious and warm-hearted people wanted to say to me. The only trouble was that my old nerves are no longer up to this kind of strain. I could not even sit down, because everybody was standing. Finally, when I saw a line of autograph hunters forming, I mumbled my apologies and fled.

I am sure I made some enemies yesterday, but it couldn't be helped. People have got to understand that it is just as bad for an old trouper's nerves to smother him with affection as it is to hoot him off the stage. I had a very bad sleep last night, and this evening I open my Eightieth Birthday Tour in Kansas City.

But first a date with the mayor of Kansas City. We met at City Hall, an impressive modern building with marble stairways, automatic elevators and streamlined offices. The mayor started off the tour by introducing me to his secretaries and assistants. Suddenly I was conscious of how tall Americans are! I am five feet ten and all the males present were taller than I. Then the mayor gave a short speech and presented me with the symbolic key to the city and a document naming me honorary citizen and assuring me that I was always welcome in Kansas City. A very friendly chap, this young mayor, like John Lindsay of New York.

During the tour of City Hall, the mayor broke into a

meeting that included a group of French engineers who had come to the United States to study American road-building techniques. He introduced me by saying, "I am sure you gentlemen know Mr. Chevalier." I told them that if they were learning as much about their specialty in the United States as I had learned about mine, they were doing very well.

I am off on the right foot! Tonight's performance in Kansas City, the first of the Eightieth Birthday Tour, was auspiciously successful. Full house, full heart.

Next stop: Independence, Missouri. Before tomorrow's plane for San José, California, I shall have the privilege of visiting former President Truman at his home.

President Truman and his wife were there to greet me at the door when I arrived. As we passed into the living room, I noticed with alarm how fragile he has become. Once he was extraordinarily strong and alert; now he seems weary, though perfectly friendly and quick to laugh. When I asked him if he spoke French as well as his daughter Margaret does, he answered, "No, I regret to say. To tell the truth, I don't even speak good English."

Before going in, we had visited the Harry S Truman Library and Museum where the former President keeps all the memorabilia from his terms of office as well as portraits and souvenirs of the Presidents who preceded him. There is even a reconstruction of his White House office. The whole collection—books, photographs, souvenirs—is displayed with typical American showmanship. *Ah, cette Amérique!*

Now that his job is done, President Truman lives surrounded by this tribute to his own legend and the glory of his country. Amazing when you think how quietly our great men disappear when their mandate is completed and are never heard from again. Clemenceau was no exception.

André Maurois just died. He was the kind of writer who will never disappear from our library shelves. A simple, outgoing man with a brilliant mind, he was truly one of the greats. When he was first stricken and taken to a clinic, I wrote him a little note wishing him a rapid recovery, and he sent me an affectionate telegram in return. Now he is no more. With a heavy heart, I have written a word of sympathy to his wife.

We are in San José, California. Box-office sales have been slow, I am told, but may pick up before the performance tomorrow. I am also told that our show is not the only one affected. Recent racial troubles have made people afraid to go out at night. Ah well, no one has ever pursued a career without running into obstacles. The important thing is not to let them stop you.

For instance, you arrive in Kansas City, where you have never set foot before. They give you the key to the city. A thousand people are turned away from your concert. President Truman receives you in his living room. Hurray for you!

And then you go to San José, California, and fall flat on your face. The vast auditorium where you perform is far from filled to capacity, and one ear has a disagreeable tendency to block up every time you sing.

But the audience is so friendly and so full of good humor that you forget your disappointment; you are delighted that at your age you can still get so much pleasure from giving pleasure. And you leave for San Francisco thanking your lucky star for letting you be the world's most dynamic going-on-eighty-year-old. Yippee! That's show business.

San Francisco looks busier and more crowded than ever. At the press conference televised from my suite at the Hilton, a reporter asked me what I thought of the suicidal tendencies among the city's hippie population. I told them about my own nervous breakdown in 1922 and about the death wish that tortured me for six months until I finally pointed a revolver at my head. Then I described the sudden flash of reason that brought me to my senses and made me put the weapon down. Obviously, then, I had no idea that the best years of my life were yet to come.

At the end of the press conference I showed everybody the little white glove that a fourteen-year-old fan had slipped into my pocket after my San José concert. I had not discovered it until I was back in my hotel room and decided on the spot that it would be my newest good-luck charm. The photographers took pictures of the glove from every conceivable angle and left with the reporters and TV cameramen. Everyone seemed satisfied.

If I want to honor all my contracts between now and 1968, I must save my strength for the moments when I am on stage. As far as my fans and the critics are concerned, it is the performance that counts. There is no point in trying to break all the endurance records in the business if they don't like what I do. Otherwise this goal of mine—to bow out in a blaze of glory—may end up being the ruin of my reputation. That is the risk I'm taking.

At last night's performance at Berkeley, California, I was pleased to see a lot of handsome young faces looking up at me. They were an enthusiastic audience, and after the show some of the girls—the cutest ones, of course—came up to kiss me. I even felt some libidinous thoughts creeping into my mind despite my vows to be forevermore pure in thought, word and deed. One of the coeds slipped a little note into my pocket that said: "Monsieur Chevalier, you are a beautiful person. You will never grow old. You will only become more beautiful."

I don't mean to sound silly, but it is little gestures like this that prove it is possible to win the affection of young people without leaving the older generation behind.

Yesterday the Hilton was the scene of a double birthday party. Every year Louis R. Lurie and I celebrate our birthdays together. We were born six days apart, seventy-nine years ago. Louis R. Lurie, "Mr. San Francisco," is the man I have always called my American Daddy (after all, he *is* six days older than I!), and this year he had organized a real extravaganza.

There were three hundred guests from all over America, the men wearing boaters with tricolor ribbons. Waiters moved among the tables singing snatches of my most popular songs. After dinner we were treated to a film made especially for this occasion showing episodes from Lurie's life—he started as a newspaper boy—and mine. The hilarious commentary was delivered by Jake Erlich, the famous lawyer, in his beautiful courtroom voice. The entertainment was accompanied by a delectable dinner à la Paris Hilton. I am not one for these American super-productions, but Louis R. Lurie is; so like a good son, I defer to my "Daddy." These occasions have all the more savor now that the relations between our two countries have become so tense.

Los Angeles. Our hotel is near the vast new Music Center where I will be singing Sunday afternoon to more than three thousand people. Some of the absentees will be the Hollywood stars who are on the beaches at Santa Monica recovering from their exhausting daily lives. Well, I understand their need for rest and excuse them. I am told that my appearance has not received much advance notice. That's all right, too. I remember what the great violinist Nathan Milstein told me once: that he wanted to live to see the day when a two-line mention of his coming in a local newspaper would fill the largest concert hall in the space of two hours. I am not quite that ambitious, but I certainly like the idea of getting a maximum return on a minimum of fanfare. There is a rumor that I will fill the house anyway. If this is the case, I will be showing Hollywood a thing or two about the rewards of discretion.

Ingrid Bergman was kind enough to get me one of the unobtainable tickets to her performance in Eugene O'Neill's *More Stately Mansions.* Still as beautiful and wholesome and gifted as ever, she has lost none of her following. The American public is usually wise in its choice of permanent favorites.

I went backstage after the play to see her in her dressing room. She confessed that she had agreed to appear in this work by O'Neill after an absence of eighteen years from the American stage because she felt her career was falling victim to her domestic happiness. With her usual frankness she remarked, "Nobody in Europe is offering me anything exciting; so I decided to come over here and see how I stood with American audiences." She has nothing to fear; her reputation is more solid than ever. This long separation from her husband, the international impresario Lars Schmidt, may be hard on both of them, but I think they were right to accept the sacrifice. That is what I told her in my thank-you letter because I suspected that this was the subject closest to her heart.

Somehow I have the feeling that they can't come to collect a man when he's singing; so even if nobody is listening, I am going to sing as long as I can.

Los Angeles gave me a marvelous reception. The audience filled the huge auditorium to the rafters and gave me three standing ovations, one at the beginning and two at the end. Los Angeles, New York and Washington are the three most important cities on my itinerary. I have made a good start.

What a crazy dream I had last night! I was back at La Louque looking at a televised tribute to Jean Gabin. Now

Jean Gabin is an actor, not a singer, but in my dream he delivered a whole series of songs in his fine deep voice. He sang with great feeling, as you might expect. I began to get worried. This fellow was going to steal my thunder right in the middle of my last big effort. Even worse, I noticed that he had shed thirty years and was as handsome as he had been when he starred in *La Grande Illusion.* I looked. I listened. And over and over I kept saying in my mind, "Come on, you guys, this isn't fair."

My left ear has a tendency to block up when I am singing, and the old mucous membranes are vibrating away. A San Francisco specialist looked at it and claimed to have licked the problem, but in Los Angeles it started acting up again. It gives me the disagreeable experience of hearing my voice in my ear; sometimes it goes away and returns when I swallow. I suspect some kind of congestion in my Eustachian tube.

I will see some more doctors, and if they can't find the trouble this affliction will have to join the group of annoying little maladies that travel around with me. I have too much to do to let it stop me. Like a matador, I will leave the ring either triumphant or dead.

October 25, 1967. A full house is awaiting me in Denver tonight. I am being as good as gold. My Eightieth Birthday Tour is the most important of my career, and I don't want to do anything to spoil it. When it's over, I am retiring to La Louque and not budging again. If they want me to make a television show or a movie, they will have to bring the cameras to my front door, or to Paris. But no farther.

The critics called last night's performance in Denver the best ever by yours truly. I am glad for them. For me it was sheer torture. Perhaps I was affected by the high altitude, though I have sung at high altitudes before. All I know is that the old man behind the jovial mask was suffering.

I am in New York, where tonight's gala April in Paris ball will honor my seventy-nine years. Back and forth, back and forth. I am overindulging in work and trips like a drunkard who has been ordered off the bottle and is spending a last night on the town. I feel the same way about my work as he feels about his pleasure. After all, when this tour is over I will have nothing to do but to sit around waiting for the Final Curtain Call. And yet I can't help feeling like an Army private at the end of his military service. Only a few more months and I'm out!

To my way of thinking, this year's April in Paris ball at the Waldorf-Astoria was not a great success. It was attended by a lot of glittering people who made a lot of noise. Even that love of a Mireille Mathieu, who was supposed to sing for them, could not get them to be quiet.

I had one agreeable surprise. Gunther Sachs, Brigitte Bardot's husband, came over to my table to say hello. He was genuinely friendly.

As the guest of honor, my duties consisted of making a short speech and introducing my little friend Mireille, and I did them as well as could be expected. Nobody is anybody at this kind of evening, and all the nobodies leave feeling worse than before.

As you may have suspected, I do not like gala evenings. I am a simple type, the man of my "one-man shows." Anything that does not go along with this side of my character makes me profoundly uneasy. When I go to noisy parties and galas, I feel like a peasant at a palace reception—that is to say, nervous and tight around the collar. The only places I really feel comfortable are at home, *chez moi,* with the people I trust, and all alone on stage. There I can be myself with a theater full of people who have come to see me, just me, my white hair, my past, my present. And perhaps my future, too.

Some finicky old craftsmen will do a job only if they can do it the way they want to. I should follow their example and do nothing that goes against my grain. No more frivolous, empty-headed parties. No more glittering galas. I should say to all those glossy people: Like me for what I am, or not at all—I don't care. But please, above all, let me be myself! Otherwise I'm lost.

This Eightieth Birthday Tour is beginning to wear me down. I try to think no further than one week ahead; otherwise I feel too tired to move or even see straight. I remind myself of the main character in Ionesco's *Le Roi se meurt* (The King Is Dying), a play I really took to heart.

Even our greatest men end up worn by overuse, or even completely on the blink. There is a limit to the length of time that you can go on being a natural wonder.

November 1, 1967. Washington seems to be in a state of nervous agitation, not at all surprising in view of the dreadful problems the whole country faces. Just last week there was a big march on the White House, the kind of thing that would have seemed inconceivable only a few months ago.

Some of the world's greatest virtuosos have performed on the stage of Constitution Hall, where I will sing tonight. Last night Leonard Bernstein and the New York Philharmonic appeared there, and even these two prestigious names were not enough to fill the hall. It seems that people are afraid to go out at night.

I had dinner last night with Senator Charles Percy and his family. He is a friend whom I respect more every time I see him. His political star is rising; who knows, someday he may be the President of the United States. Unfortunately I see no one of his stature among the young politicos of France.

Also yesterday, a Washington broadcasting station telecast a party in my honor. I was flattered to see that some very prominent people had come to congratulate me and show me their affection, Senator Percy among them. We all partook of an enormous cake and French champagne flown over especially. Especially for the occasion, ladies and gentlemen!

The tenderness that this tough country has shown me really warms my heart. Once I was a fifteen-year-old kid who dreamed of nothing but American boxers, American dancers, American music. And will you look at me now? The fairy tale has come true for one Paris street kid as a reward for his labor of love.

Constitution Hall exploded last night—with affection. If only for the memories it will leave me, this tour was the right thing to do.

Now we are in Pittsburgh, cold and humid. I feel drained and exhausted, and I am going to bed. My tour fills me with apprehension: all those airplane flights, all those interviews, all those one-night stands.

The malaise that is affecting America has started to affect me, too. It has gotten on my nerves, like the humidity and fatigue. Here in Pittsburgh, too, people are afraid to go out at night, and the high schools are occupied by the police because of racial tension.

And yet I am making progress; seven cities down, twelve more to go. Sure, my legs are tired, but I would rather have tired legs than no legs at all. Sure, I am under the weather, but at least I am not under the ground.

By curtain time I had recovered enough to give total satisfaction to the three thousand people who filled Pittsburgh's Penn Hall. Obviously this provincial city is not used to the sight of a foreigner in his eightieth year taking over a whole stage for a one-man show. Now let's see what Buffalo thinks.

Bad weather is bad anywhere on the globe except in America. There it is worse. American humidity is a real depressant; it makes you feel empty and weak, and you stay that way until the weather changes. But on the bad days, you really feel lousy—or as we say in Paris, *foutu*.

Buffalo is cold. An icy blast is going "hoo, hoo" just like the wind in horror films.

My age is not the only thing handicapping this tour. There is also the problem of the bad social climate in America. In almost every city we have visited so far, crime has caused people to lock themselves in after dark, and there are ten more cities to go in this first leg of the Eightieth Birthday Tour. But we have passed the halfway mark. The success of the first half has convinced me that it was a good idea to come. For the second half, like anybody and everybody, I count on the good Lord's help.

Buffalo's snowy weather was as bad for ticket sales as it was for my old throat. Happily the press liked my performance. Now on to Ottawa to see if the English Canadians have any appetite left for old Frenchmen after *le grand Charles'* visit.

My motor is beginning to grumble but at least it continues to turn over. I remind myself of the old nags around 1900 that pulled the busses from the Montparnasse train station up to Ménilmontant, where I was born and lived as a boy. Those horses had to go on working until they no longer had the energy to make the last grade and fell—often never to rise again—just short of the terminal. Only I have not fallen yet and continue to clop along like a good old dobbin.

A funny coincidence: my appearance in Ottawa is sold out for tonight, and Charles Aznavour is sold out in Ottawa for tomorrow. One of our greatest vocalists, he has had trouble with his health. I admire his guts and determination and the results he gets.

Ottawa was a smash success. This morning I awoke to find the city buried under a blanket of snow. I wonder if we will be able to take off for Toronto.

I am beginning to adopt the attitude of a kid in the military service: I let events take their course. My approach is due half to fatalism, half to fatigue. Everything's O.K.? O.K. Everything's not O.K.? Too bad. Whatever happens, I go on doing my tricks like a trained animal. I come on stage, I sit up and beg, the audience claps (that's my reward), and then I go back in the cage again until the next performance. This is my life, and I like it better than any other I can think of.

Although Ottawa was more than sold out, Toronto, not far from the Canadian capital, was less than full. Why? It would be one of those show-business mysteries if it were not for the fact that Prince Philip, Queen Elizabeth's husband, gave a gala dinner in Toronto last night that preempted some of my public. Luckily, quantity doesn't necessarily mean quality, and my Toronto audience was a good one. Everywhere I go, I get the same enthusiastic reception. This Eightieth Birthday Tour is one for the books.

The places, mostly in the provinces, where I no longer fill a theater are like memories that are fading away. People who used to come to hear me now seek their entertainment elsewhere. They have seen me and heard me so much that they no longer get my message. These are disappointments that I must learn to accept. When people forget me, I must forget them, too, so that I can do my best by the friends and fans I have left. And if somebody else wants to leave the fold, he should be allowed to go in peace. My arms should be wide open to receive but not to detain.

I will have to learn to put things in perspective. When the tour is over with, I will never darken all these concert halls again. The last page of my show-business history will have been written. Even I shall start to forget some of it, hopefully not the best parts but the failures, the disappointments, the cold goodbyes. I must be sure not to burden myself with a lot of regrets.

See, dear Ionesco, your play has taught me a great deal. It shows me that if I want to die honestly and well, I must keep looking not downward but upward. Downward, there is the ground where I will molder and all the other reminders of what is soon to come. But upward, beyond the clouds and the smog, is freedom. Or at least that's what we hope.

I am in Philadelphia and have just returned from a window-shopping tour of the city's big department stores. On my way I ran into some teenagers waving their arms and talking loudly and a group of blacks that looked as if they were out on a reconnaissance mission. The dirty sidewalks made quite a contrast to the opulent displays in the windows. Sometimes older people passed me, alone or in couples. They looked embarrassed to be old, or well off, or both.

Tomorrow I sing. Tonight I am in bed watching a couple of polished professionals, Jackie Gleason and Lawrence Welk, do their attractive TV shows.

Speaking of television, I have just had some good news. The show that I prepared before I left with J. C. Averty and Diahann Carroll has been televised, and it met with great enthusiasm in France. I am delighted and relieved. I was beginning to get nervous about appearing before my compatriots. So many of them are young and eager to cut themselves loose from all the old traditions. I am afraid they will think I have delusions of grandeur.

Of course I have decided to take that risk. Anyone who wants to break records knows he is courting disaster; but if you were in my place, wouldn't you do the same thing? I am the type of person who will quit only when I am down, and even then I might bounce right up again.

I was particularly moved by my reception in Philadelphia because I recognize its high and historic status among American cities. The show was sold out. After the performance the mayor of Philadelphia came up on stage to present me with a letter stamped with the seal of the city naming me an example to the young. And the cheers of the audience were still ringing in my ears as I set off for the next stop on my American marathon.

They don't believe it when I say goodbye. Or when I say that I am going to relegate the boater to a hatbox and start to take care of myself. Or that this is my last burst of energy before calling it quits. Perhaps their disbelief is my fault. I keep trying to give the impression that doing an Eightieth Birthday Tour is the easiest thing in the world.

South Burlington, Vermont. The snow is coming down in great big flakes. I think I will stay in my hotel room until it's time to sing.

Sometimes I wonder, in the days when I am no longer performing, how I will be able to serve the public that has done so much for me. I am going to have to confer with myself in the weeks following my last recital. Resting on my show-business laurels will never satisfy me; there will have to be more to my life than that. Perhaps when I am done polishing my performances I can go to work on my record as a human being.

The Cardinal and Archbishop of Montreal, Monsignor Paul-Émile Léger, has just set an example for all of us. At the end of his career he has cast off his robes and his honors to go work as a simple missionary in an African leper colony. He explained that he thought the time had come to practice what he preached. Or as he put it, "I do not think that being a cardinal should prevent you from doing good."

Translated into my terms that means, "It is not too bad to be stingy if you can be more generous later on." I have already tried to improve myself in the generosity department. From time to time I have gone to see old friends who have fallen on hard times. They are delighted to have a visitor and to pass the time of day and can't believe their eyes when they find a small fortune in their palms after our last handshake. Then we begin to cry like children—they because they need the money so much, and me because I need it so little and am so glad to make them happy.

That is the kind of satisfaction I would like to give more of when my warbling days are over. All my life I have been accused of being a penny-pincher. I'll show 'em! It tickles me just to think about it.

The temperature in South Burlington is well below zero, and the town is buried under a blanket of snow and ice. Still, not a single person stayed away from my concert. Every one of the 2,400 seats in the university theater was taken.

I wish I could go on forever.

As usual, my audience in New Haven bridged the generations. I was especially touched to see all the students who had put down their books to come to hear me sing.

New Haven is on its way to becoming one of America's most modern cities. Some of the big stores rival Fifth Avenue, and in the arcades each new little shop is more tempting than the last. I also appreciated the buildings of Yale University. Too bad that my "Hello, New Haven, pleased to meet you" was also a "Goodbye."

Some minor indispositions had me afraid for a minute, but my lucky star was with me on the night of the concert. My triumph set me up for the rest of the tour.

November 19, 1967. Last night I sang at Philharmonic Hall in New York's Lincoln Center. The world's most modern and prestigious hall was sold out to the last seat, including the five hundred extra chairs set up on the stage. And what's more, I managed this feat with a minimum of advance publicity. My arrival in New York was so unheralded that I wondered for a minute if I hadn't left America. No telephone calls. Two telegrams. Deathly silence.

And then, all of a sudden, there was the crowd closing in on me after the performance in a great big hug of affection. Their enthusiasm almost suffocated me, literally and figuratively. And the review in this morning's *New York Times* is headlined "Chevalier Glows at Philharmonic." Last night's performance was another jewel in my crown. But I'd better not gloat about it; I have too much left to do. I can only say that the loving reception New York gave me is indelibly written on my heart and also on the pages of show-business history.

I am cross. An Albany reporter whom I spoke to when I arrived has me saying in this morning's paper that I hate rock-'n'-rollers. That is not what I said. I said that I didn't see how they could last very long. In fact the whole article is rather nasty; it starts off by quoting Coco Chanel to the effect that I should have retired years ago. After that, I'll be surprised if there is a person under thirty in my Albany audience.

Last night I watched myself in color on American television. The program was filmed at La Louque and shows me strolling through the house and garden singing twenty of my most popular songs. Now let me tell you my impressions.

I saw a kind of singing actor who basically is neither an actor nor a singer, but rather an attractive old man. He walks more slowly than he used to, but his face still reflects inner freshness and youth. As for his delivery, it has more sincerity than technical perfection.

Sincerity. That is my biggest value as a performer, and that is what keeps people coming to hear me.

Reviews: The bad ones sometimes do me good, the good ones sometimes are bad for me. But as long as my public sticks by me, I won't ask myself too many questions. Who knows if there are any answers? Public preferences are shrouded in mystery, like a woman past her prime who continues to be desirable.

I am told that Albany is a state capital. It certainly doesn't look like one; it looks like a little provincial city, a big Small Town, U.S.A. The people in the movie theater where I performed were friendly and unaffected. They received my show enthusiastically and so did the press.

Mission accomplished.

Indianapolis is next on the docket, and it has not been easy to get here. First of all, our departure was delayed for an hour because of engine trouble on the plane. Then at Kennedy Airport, where we were supposed to change planes, the runways were overloaded with Thanksgiving traffic. We came down in a pea-soup fog so thick I marveled that the pilot could find the runway. After more delays, the plane for Indianapolis took off. When we got to Indianapolis, we did some more turning and waiting in another pea-soup fog. Finally we landed. Whew!

Under these conditions you begin to realize the uncertainty of all human planning that depends on the airplane. I have gotten fatalistic about the whole business, and my companions, the Vals and Fred Freed, my accompanist, follow me around like three brave soldiers who assume that their leader knows where he is going.

Only too often modern architects pamper the public when they design theaters and forget the fellow behind the curtain. Not in Indianapolis. The handsome auditorium where I sang last night has everything a performer could ask for in his dressing room: toilet, shower, spacious closets. Thank you, sirs.

We are in Midland, Michigan, staying at a country club whose broad lawns and trees hold a promise of peace and quiet. The first leg of my Eightieth Birthday Tour is almost over; after St. Louis and Atlanta we go back to La Louque. So far I think the tour has been an unqualified success, especially considering all the troubles that are keeping Americans out of theaters.

I wonder what I was thinking of when I planned this tour? Did I realize how risky it was to pawn off a simple little show like mine on people who are used to modern show-business techniques in orchestration, lighting and so forth? And what about the strain? Maybe I decided I wouldn't really deserve the Big Sleep until I was thoroughly exhausted.

And look what has happened: I have triumphed everywhere. Perhaps you are beginning to think that I am pretty repetitious, but, you know, the end is coming and I want to square with myself. When I started out in this profession, all I wanted was to earn an honest living. I never thought I would go much farther than that because everyone around was so much more talented than I. Every year, though, my determination brought me up a notch, and now look! Here I am in my eightieth year breaking show-business records, and all because long ago America accepted me as I am and gave me its encouragement, even though I seem like an ordinary person next to its flamboyant stars.

That's where the real miracle comes in, and that's what makes me think I can be an inspiration for other kids who are starting out poor in slums and ghettos all over the world. Because there is no secret to my success. My principle virtues have always been simplicity, guts, kindness and good humor, and they still are.

Everywhere I go people ask me to come back. If I let them, the Americans would extend my tour by a dozen years or so.

Many of the students and their families who came to see me last night in a Midland auditorium told me afterward that they were watching me live for the very first time. Most of them had seen me only in the movies or on television.

Six days from now I land at Orly, a tired old boy who started out behind and has more than caught up. Sometimes I feel like an old ballet star who has danced on the world's greatest stages and is still in demand even though he does his entrechats with a cane.

Goodbye, Midland. I have enjoyed this restful place that seemed like a calm interlude in Chevalier's Last Stand.

St. Louis, we find, is having its face lifted. It has even acquired its own Eiffel Tower in the form of a monumental arch. The mayor of the city gave me a pretty little model of it along with the key to the city. Two nice souvenirs.

My performance at the Kiel Auditorium was to benefit a new monastery and its charitable works. Three thousand people paid the price to see me, and they all seemed to think that they had gotten their money's worth.

Atlanta, Georgia—last stop before La Louque. It is going to be hard to keep Georgia on my mind.

The hotel I'm staying at—the Regency Hyatt House—will help. It is the most fabulously modern yet, a real tribute to the American taste and ingenuity that continue to prevail even in this time of troubles. What a country!

The newspapers give more and more space to the growing disagreements between France and America. When reporters ask me about the subject, I say that I don't follow politics and am not equipped to answer; that all of us in France hope that General de Gaulle knows what he is doing and that we are confident nothing permanently damaging can come between two countries who have loved and respected each other since the time of Lafayette.

I am certainly not the first Frenchman to have fears for the future, but I am the last to be able to discuss the present knowledgeably. My whole career has been a labor of love in which politics played no part. I'm the oldest hippie going; I'm a simple sunshine salesman. What do they want?

The hall I am singing in tonight seats 5,500 people and is used for sporting events, concerts and political conventions. What a contrast you find in these American cities! Atlanta has the most up-to-date hotels and public buildings imaginable but has yet to build a concert hall in keeping with the rest.

My press conference was well received. Paul Hemphill's column was headlined, "Thank Heaven for Chevalier," and then went on to say, ". . . ask how Americans would feel about France if it were not for one man, and the man's name is Maurice Chevalier."

The Americans of the present day are a strong and sensitive people who are beginning to lose patience, like a good giant who is being taunted by the people he has helped.

Marnes-la-Coquette, January 1, 1968. It is four weeks since I got back from my two-month tour of twenty-two American cities. The moment I got home I had to begin work on the second side, the one in English, of a special record in honor of my eightieth year. I didn't even have time to adjust to the six hours' difference between France and America, and the result is that I caught a first-class cold and had to resort to antibiotics. I was so tired and nervous that I was unable to sleep more than two or three hours a night. Soon my old fears and complexes reached crisis proportions. My next tour, through England and Scandinavia, loomed up before me and I couldn't see how I was going to make it through my international goodbyes.

Slowly I began to regain confidence and my near-nervous breakdown became part of the past. Now it is the first day of 1968, well into my eightieth year. America, step number one, is already in the bag (though I return to do a few more cities later in the year). As far as the next laps are concerned, I will just keep on going until I run out of breath.

I have come to Knokke, Belgium, to spend a long weekend with my friends the Nellens, directors of the Casino. Rain and wind ushered in this month of January, but so did warmth and friendship. Now that I am here, I am going to see my old friend Prince Charles, Count of Flanders, the only person of royal blood I know well.

I also want to see General Lemnitzer, commander of the Allied Forces in Europe, who used to be my neighbor in Marnes-la-Coquette until politics intervened and General Lemnitzer and SHAPE moved to Belgium. He sent me a two-page handwritten Christmas letter this year. It was so affectionate and free of rancor that I could feel a lump rising in my throat while I read it. As I have said, I stay away from politics. But I don't think anyone will hold it against me if I express my thanks to America and Americans for what they have done for me. America was the great adventure of my professional life, and I couldn't look myself in the face if I didn't admit the extent of my affection and gratitude.

"My" prince just paid us the honor of coming to lunch at the Réserve with his lovely young companion Karin. Gustave Nellens has set aside a room in his hotel for occasions like this and has decorated it royally. We had a pleasant lunch there and then moved on to Gustave's apartment so that the Prince could meet his family. After several hours, during which we all did our utmost to please him, the Prince left for home, quite obviously enchanted. We were happy, too, to have given him such a good time.

Unfortunately I couldn't see General Lemnitzer because he was leaving for Bonn. So all we could do was to express our mutual regret at not being able to have a neighborly visit.

For the last few days I have been indulging myself in vodka, champagne and sherry. The only result is that I can see I am in no danger of becoming alcoholic. Not while my French liver is in me to sound out alarms and while I still remember the sad sight of admirable people I know who have had too much to drink.

The sea air in Knokke is just what the doctor ordered as far as my breathing apparatus is concerned. It is a cold and rainy Sunday and I am going to take a long walk. The time has come to clear my head and start thinking about what I am going to sing for them in Scandinavia and England.

Just as I wrote these words sitting up in bed, the sun broke through the clouds and looked at me through the window as if to say, "You spoke too soon!" Sorry, Mr. Sunshine. I was just pretending that I could do without you, and you know and I know I can't.

My companion Félix Paquet may not look very strong, but he has a will of iron. He knows instinctively what is good for him and what is not. Whenever he is offered alcohol, rich foods, things like that, he can brush away temptation with a flick of the hand.

Félix is an exemplary companion and, while I am on the subject, my best audience too. There is a philosophical side to his nature that I greatly appreciate. Félix was not always the man he is today. When he was young, he shared all the foibles of the social and professional crowds he ran around with; then he abandoned them, apparently none the worse for the experience. It has been comforting to have someone as talented and wise as Félix to rely on. Sometimes I am not sure who is stronger—me or Félix my disciple!

I never get tired of La Louque, our friendly "family" suppers, our expeditions into Paris for Sunday matinees.

This is what we have seen since I got home: the French production of *Black Comedy*, with wonderful Jean-Pierre Cassel and Raymond Gérôme and the adorable new star Marlène Jobert; and *L'Escalier*, a translation of the English *Staircase*, with Paul Meurisse and Daniel Ivernel playing two aging homosexuals who introduce us to their eccentric little world, so moving that often you can't decide whether to laugh or to cry. Then, at the Théâtre de la Porte Saint-Martin, the remarkable comic duo Roger Pierre and Jean-Marc Thibault; and at the Nouveautés, Annie Cordy and Darry Cowl, two great comedians united under the same roof. And last but not least, Henri de Montherlant's monumental *La Ville dont le Prince est un enfant* (The City Whose Prince Is a Child) that proves once again his genius for portraying the heights and depths of human feeling. *Quelle richesse française!*

I also went to check up on my protégée Mireille Mathieu at the Olympia, the citadel of pop song. She has made a lot of progress and has lost none of her lovely freshness while she was at it. All she needs now is the feeling and experience being a woman will give her. I have confidence that she will grow, professionally and personally; meanwhile she represents the best of French youth for the public at large.

I have just been to the annual dinner at Ris-Orangis, the old home for entertainers that has always been my most important "good work." This time I had the melancholy task of renouncing my title of Honorary President and passing it on to Charles Aznavour. In my speech I recalled the whole history of my association with the home, my campaigns for it, the bogus boxing matches I put on for it (some of them turned out to be not so bogus!), my efforts to serve it in every way I could. Then I closed by explaining all the reasons why Charles Aznavour was the right person to replace me and told the assembly that, as far as I was concerned, they could place their faith in him.

The group rose in honor of their new Honorary President, whom I presented with considerable emotion. My heart was heavy as I drove back to La Louque. One burden less, it's true; but also one more sacrifice.

Before I left for Scandinavia, I went to see Aznavour performing at the Olympia and asked him to bring his family to lunch.

Charles Aznavour is a unique case in our world of song. He is always moving ahead, whether in his work or in his personal life, and he always seems to let his own intelligence be his guide. I find he has more class every time I see him.

Already he is perfectly outspoken about the fact that he is not getting any younger. More than any other singer, perhaps, he can tell us how to grow old. He is most moving when he is on stage and most congenial when he is at table. An enchanting fellow.

We arrived in Helsinki in a snowstorm. Luckily, a freezing spell in Paris had already prepared us for the shock of the northern cold. The manager of the theater where I was to sing greeted us at the airport with the cheerful announcement that all the tickets to my concert were sold a couple of hours after the box office opened. Either I have become a complete fatalist or I am a pushover for theaters filled with my fans. In any event, I picked up the threads again after my long vacation with such ease that even I was amazed. When I had taken my last bows before a wildly enthusiastic audience, the manager came up on stage to ask me to do a farewell performance every year. Never, he said, had France sent a better ambassador to Finland.

I did not even have any lapses of memory, or the hesitations you might expect of an old man going on eighty who has every reason to feel tired. You would have thought I'd had a new brain—or a computer, maybe—installed in my head while I was back in Paris.

Time to leave for Stockholm. Get moving, old boy. Let's show the world that your heart is one organ that doesn't need replacing.

My first farewell show in Stockholm ended in a whirlwind of affection that I thought never would put me down again. The theater was jammed with people from Swedish show business, my managers past and present, members of the French colony in Sweden and many, many more.

After the performance they came up on stage one after another bearing flowers, gifts, official decorations. Each new presentation was heralded by a row of trumpeters, and the audience was on its feet shouting out hurrahs. I have never experienced anything like it, either in France or America. Half an hour after the end of my show I was still up on stage racking my brain to think of new ways to thank them. The French Ambassador to Sweden (who has invited us to lunch) came to congratulate me in my dressing room, looking a bit overwhelmed by what he had just seen.

The second night's audience was more controlled but just as happy. This time a lot of young people had come to say goodbye. My admiration for this handsome race of people makes me value their affection for me all the more.

Monsieur André Puget, the French Ambassador to Sweden, is much more natural and friendly than most people in the diplomatic profession, and his wife is too. At their lunch for me they had assembled artists and performers from France and Sweden, and we all drank "skoals" to Franco-Swedish friendship. I have always felt that Stockholm loved me all the more because I was French; so this was a fitting finale to my Stockholm farewells.

After lunch at the French Embassy I took one last stroll around this friendly city, a kind of pilgrimage to the spots I had fallen in love with on previous tours. More and more I feel the need to revisit the sites of pleasant moments in my life. This could prove to be my most pleasant pastime when I have retired from the stage. My whole life would unreel before my eyes: I would relive the progress of little Maurice from Ménilmontant to fame and reassure myself that he could not have done better.

Perhaps my new hobby will teach me to take courage from my own example and finish my life simply and well.

I am counting on this basic simplicity of mine to help me look back on my life with a smile and prepare myself for the visit from the Lady in Black. You will probably laugh when I tell you that I would not mind at all if they broadcast the crucial moment on color television. That way I could say one last goodbye to my international public and then turn over, pink-cheeked and cheerful, for the eternal sleep.

February 1, 1968. I am in Göteborg, Sweden, a city that has been greatly modernized since I was last here twelve years ago. A wonderful reception with a tinge of melancholy to it: perhaps because my Göteborg public and I have changed together, aged together, and now are coming to the end of our association together.

Copenhagen is all decked out to celebrate the marriage of one of Denmark's princesses to her handsome German. For obvious reasons it did not pay too much attention to my arrival in the middle of the preparations. I was fortunate enough to perform to a full house of elegant people at the Tivoli Theater yesterday. Will I be as lucky tonight? I do not presume to compete with the deep affection the Danes feel for their royal family. Amidst all these trappings and symbols of devotion I feel very small, very ordinary. I'm Momo again. I'm going to have lunch now at the Embassy—a bit deflated, but relieved somehow to have regained a certain sense of perspective.

Not a big city anyway, Copenhagen is glued to a man to its television sets. From dawn to dusk the Danes are following the ceremony surrounding the royal marriage. Result: A sparse attendance at my second farewell show. But those who came gave me an affectionate goodbye.

Vienna is shrouded in a cold and hostile fog, and I am glad not to be a tourist. At the Hotel Imperial I have been given a suite that looks like something Ernst Lubitsch would have put me in for my old hit movie *Love Parade.* I can tell you I feel foolish in it!

Tomorrow I sing here and then go on to Amsterdam. We are halfway through the second leg of the Eightieth Birthday Tour. I have decided that there will be two more stops before I wrap it up with a series of recitals at the Théâtre des Champs-Élysées in Paris, around the end of September '68, the month of my eightieth birthday.

Am I going to make it that far? Only fate will decide. One thing is sure though: stepping down after Paris will not be too painful. I want to live out the rest of my life at home as best I can, but at least in peace and quiet. I want the old age of gentleman artist, philosopher and philanthropist who has come to terms with himself. That is by far the most graceful way to die, but it does not come without self-knowledge. My career will be well in the bag by that time, but I can still tarnish the memory of it, and me, by some parting folly.

I know, I am beginning to talk too much about the problem of my exit, but it is the only future I have to discuss. It's so important to me to leave the table before I end up under it!

A stupendous evening at the Vienna Konzerthaus—too stupendous in fact. I have found that I can still take the performances but not the frenzy that surrounds them: the press conferences, the radio and TV interviews, the rush of people backstage after my last bow. They invade my dressing room, take pictures, ask for autographs, talk and gesticulate around me and at me, and I begin to panic. This is a nightmare that repeats itself at each recital. Maybe I am psychologically unequipped to keep up with the evolution of the times, or maybe I should have a bodyguard like the modern-day idols.

The fact remains that Vienna gave me a memorable reception. And I gave my morale another lift by going out and buying five Habig hats to wow people on the Champs-Élysées.

My next stop was Amsterdam, where I had sung only twice before, once in 1936 and again around 1956. Despite our infrequent get-togethers, Amsterdam treated me like an old friend. It's the same story everywhere. In city after city, people come to thank me for spending my life making them happy. If I have any lingering traces of fatigue left over from one performance, the burst of affection after the next one wipes it away. All this enthusiasm may be the death of me, but if I have to die, this is the way to do it.

We are getting ready to leave for London. It is a critical moment in English history, and I hope the country doesn't take out its frustrations on me. Somehow I have got to let people know that I will never forget my debt of gratitude to England, one of my earliest supporters, no matter how tangled Anglo-French relations become.

London: The foggy city, scene of my first flights of inspiration as a performer. The minute I got here I took a leisurely stroll around the city to see what has happened to it in my four years' absence. The West End, Piccadilly Circus and Leicester Square have not improved; if anything, they are more garish and aggressive than before. The rest of London seems to have kept its traditional aloofness, as if it is deliberately unaware of what the eccentric minority of Londoners are up to.

I am told that everything looks fine for my English concerts, including of course the one in London. Only six more to go and the second leg of the Eightieth Birthday Tour is over, after thirty-six concerts and (it would appear) thirty-six triumphs, proving that at almost eighty years of age I can still travel the world with my one-man show and be successful everywhere. And I do it empty-handed, with no sham, nothing up my sleeve. This is an indisputable plus in my credit column for the hour of reckoning.

The photographers and reporters at my Sunday press conference in London gave me such a cold reception that I practically shivered. For a moment I thought that my worst fears were realized; they were really holding me responsible for French policy toward England. Just then the lights went into action, the TV cameras started grinding away, flashbulbs popped and questions started coming at me thick and fast. While I was answering them, as honestly as possible, I slowly became aware that things had started to thaw. We parted on the best of terms, and now all this morning's papers show that I am the darling of the English press.

February 14, 1968. My English tour opened in a Manchester movie house, where I had some trouble warming people up. It took me four songs to get them going, and then from that time on it was smooth sailing all the way.

So the English tour has started off well, and further encouraging news comes from London, where the Palladium concert is already sold out.

Reporters here still ask me about my political opinions, the way they do everywhere. My answer never changes. I always tell them that as far as I am concerned, my job is to make people forget for a while that things like politics exist, and that regardless of what others may have said or thought, I have never given my support to left, right or center. If some people want to devote their lives to this kind of activity, that's their business. Mine is to sing and smile at everybody, whatever his politics.

But you can't stop the English from feeling that the French don't like them, and of course that kind of thing doesn't help the rapport between a performer and his public. So you can imagine how elated I was when I read a review in an English paper that said, "There will never be another Frenchman like M.C.," and added, "but then, there never was."

I am as nervous as a debutante. Tomorrow night is the big concert at the London Palladium, and London has become so important in world show business that if I flop here, I might as well call it quits on the whole Eightieth Birthday Tour.

Tell me, why have I always insisted on doing things the hard way? Because I do not want to owe my success to anyone or anything. I want to be my own man, free of "connections" and fads.

I feel better after a good sleep. We have been at the Palladium setting up for tonight and I find the theater less problematical than many. The tiers rise very high, and if there is any trouble, that is where it will come from. London audiences, and especially the people in the balconies, can be cruel and heartless; I still remember one opening night in 1925 (the unfortunate play was called *White Birds*) when two-thirds of the show was drowned out by boos and catcalls. By some miracle I was spared the general sarcasm, but an evening like that sticks in your craw. Well, I can't turn back now! I have to confront the London of miniskirts and

Beatlemania with my white hair and my simple little show.

Tonight will either be the night of nights or the day Chevalier hit the dust. I am praying to the Lord, I am praying to La Louque. O.K., Momo, this is it!

I did it. A simple music-hall public at the London Palladium has just given me an evening so charged with emotion and satisfaction that it can only be called colossal. With tears in its eyes and a lump in its throat, London has said goodbye. As for me, I will remember this evening until my dying smile.

The critics are unanimous in deciding that I have passed with flying colors. I can relax. I am coming into the home stretch without a competitor in sight—if there ever was one. And if there are some about to appear on the horizon? I wish them luck, but they are no concern of mine.

My only worry now is making sure that my popularity doesn't go to my head. I want to conclude my tour simply and without striving for effect. Until I retire, my performances should be my only justification; afterward I can rest on my laurels, not before. And by then it will be time to be quiet and let other people talk.

It was snowing when we arrived in Glasgow. I spent most of the night shivering and thinking I was about to come down with something. Took my temperature this morning: no fever. I decided that it must be my liver, a Frenchman's gastronomic conscience, telling me to stop drinking to my victories, even in moderation. Soon I am going to be as lucid about my failings as our late great writer André Gide.

Tonight I sing in a movie theater seating 2,700 people. I don't like those places. They are difficult to perform in and they have no atmosphere. But after my reception in London, I have no right to complain.

Poor Mireille Mathieu. Our young and talented little vocalist is beginning to pay the price for her miraculous rise to fame in the form of anonymous letters that threaten murder, kidnaping, anything that sick minds can think of. And now she has just had a second automobile accident that could have been fatal. It wasn't, but she was badly enough hurt for her doctors to put her to bed for several months. Fate is beginning to play games with this pretty, hard-working child. She will win out in the end, though; you can tell from the determined set to her chin. She has moral and physical strength on her side. A real little champion.

Glasgow engulfed me in the same wave of enthusiasm that has swept all of England. A national hero could not have asked for more. No sooner have I received one ovation than I set off for another—in this case, Cardiff's. (I hope you like airchair travel.)

Same story there. The tension that exists today between our two countries makes these emotional farewells all the more touching. One problem: For no reason at all —you know I never touch politics—people are saying that I do not approve of you-know-who's policy toward England. If you-know-who hears this rumor, I hope he doesn't believe it. If I get the whole French government mad at me, I may lose my function as the guardian angel of the Entente Cordiale.

We are off to Coventry, terminus for the English tour. A thousand thoughts are running through my head at the same time, dominated by a desire to finish things up in style.

Who says that not taking part in politics is a political stance? It is possible to sing through and above all political winds, and I am here to prove it.

Coventry, one of the martyred cities of the last war, has now been almost entirely rebuilt in modern style. New store windows, bright-looking kids. In their superb new theater, the citizens of Coventry and I came together to say goodbye. The next morning's papers refused to believe the evidence. Why do I call this my swan song, they ask, when I still have so much to give? Now that it is time to part, provincial England opens its arms wider to me than ever before.

Now I go back to La Louque, vastly encouraged by my success in the most "with it" capital of the show-business world and my reception in the smaller English cities that are usually so resistant to things foreign. If the England of the Beatles can still get my message, then I was absolutely right not to step down earlier. Thank you, Albion; your praises are not falling on deaf ears. I am going home full of hope for all my projects, for television, the movies, the stage.

I slipped back into France on tiptoe and sneaked back to La Louque. What a surprise after all those performances to find myself in the bosom of my "family" for a quiet few weeks!

I immediately went to see Mireille Mathieu in her sickbed. It is easy to see that she has been affected by this latest shock; she has gotten too thin, her pretty little face has a yellowish tinge, her tiny hands lie white on her covers. She responded in a hollow voice to my attempts to give her courage. A photographer and reporter from the newspaper *France-Soir* were there and asked if they could have a picture of the two of us together. Permission granted. I left her after half an hour's visit, and the next day most of the front page of *France-Soir* was taken up by the picture of Mireille with me at her bedside.

Mireille is strong. She will recover.

Had a visit with my doctors, who saw no reason for me to slow down for the moment. I am operating on energy and luck. The thought of hanging up the boater is occupying me more and more.

I have been asked to say a few words on the radio about Frank Sinatra. There is so much to say. He is unique in our profession for the breadth of his talent. The personality, the voice, the much imitated style, the smile that can run from hot to cold, all of these assets helped him to his triumph as a singer and then guaranteed his success as an actor on the screen. What's more, he has the guts and brains of a tycoon. He can direct and produce as well as act and sing—in short, he is the biggest bundle of talents in American show biz. Needless to say, I admire him immensely.

Just recently a record company brought out an album which brings together all my American hits of the 1930s. I don't mean to sound sentimental, but I had tears in my eyes listening to those rhythms, those orchestrations and —*pardonnez-moi*—my way of singing those songs. Why? Well, because I could tell why America loved me. Old fans who hear this record will relive their youths; newcomers, I hope, will be inspired by it. As for me, I see why I clicked and why doors all over the world opened for me.

The manager of Manitas de Plata, the recently discovered Spanish guitarist, asked me to contribute a few lines to the program to be used for his appearances. And here they are:

Manitas de Plata. An appealing tanned face, with a naturalness which immediately strikes you. A divine fire burns in his eyes, his heart and his fingertips and sets his instrument and his music ablaze. And yet it is rare in our times to find someone as human and unaffected as he is. *Olé,* Manitas de Plata.

The third lap of my Eightieth Birthday Tour is about to begin. My stay in Paris has been so brief that all I can remember is fleeting impressions. At least they are happy ones:

Sunday lunch at La Louque.

The actor Robert Lamoureux joining the ranks of the "greats" of popular comedy. Michel Bouquet in *Pauvre Bitos.* Hearing our fine actor Serge Reggiani sing. The modern, muscular humor of *Adieu Berthe* with Francis Blanche and company. The show at the Folies-Bergère.

And, of course, my strolls through Paris, my pilgrimages to Ménilmontant chasing down old memories.

Happy parties at La Louque.

The time has gone too fast. We are packing again.

And always the nagging thought that soon this way of life is coming to an end; that another will take its place that will make me a different kind of person; and that in spite of this change, I must still fulfill the demands that I make of myself.

Let it happen. I am ready.

April 5, 1968. President Johnson has announced that he will not run again and that he has ordered negotiations to begin concerning the war in Vietnam.

In Memphis, Martin Luther King has shared the fate of President Kennedy. He is dead, assassinated, and the whole world is shocked. We are glued to radio and television, all asking the same question: Will there be a civil war?

I am due to leave for Florida shortly, and as long as America does not go up in flames, I will be there to honor my contracts. We are still packing our bags. I rehearse with Fred Freed. Nobody must suspect that we are the slightest bit afraid. *Courage, mes amis.*

The day after tomorrow we leave for the United States, where the situation looks bad. The black leader Stokely Carmichael has declared war on the whites and civil war threatens many American cities. Blacks are pillaging and attacking whites whether they are racist or not. Washington looks like an armed camp, and the White House is on the verge of calling in the National Guard for its own protection.

We go on packing our bags. Our arrival is scheduled for the day of Martin Luther King's funeral in Atlanta.

Some say that President Johnson will be there and that flags will be flown at half mast all over America. As for us, we arrive in New York in the middle of the afternoon. We will be met at the airport by Sol Shapiro of the William Morris Agency, who organized my tour. French radio has just announced that houses are burning in Baltimore, Pittsburgh, Washington and Chicago. Friends call me up and tell me that I'm crazy to go. America is blowing up, they say. You can't even get insurance for your trip; no company would sell it to you. Don't be a martyr. Stay at La Louque!

I listen, and then I think of all I owe that wonderful country. Surely Americans will know how I feel about them if they see me and my eighty years coming over there to cheer them up. And if I die—well, I will just be showing everybody a new way to die for love. I am almost happy to be going. I am going to hit those troubled shores crying out, "Here I come, America!"

And, of course, I am not going over there to fight. I am going over there to smile, to shake hands, to sing about friendship. Poor giant of a country, it is really suffering. Once upon a time it thought it could save the world, and now it can barely save itself.

Mireille got up from her sickbed for the first time today to come to La Louque and say hello, goodbye. She was taking things very carefully and had to lean on someone's arm—in this case, mine—to walk. I think she's out of danger, but I certainly lifted my old eyebrows when she told me that she is doing a one-nighter at the London Palladium a short two weeks from now.

Are those two thin little legs going to be able to carry her onto the stage and off it again? I guess they have no choice. Good luck, Mireille, wonderful little kid that you are. Just a short while ago you were safe in the bosom of the family Mathieu in Avignon with your thirteen brothers and sisters; and now, already, you are the target of jealousy and hate because of your success.

"Heavy Calm Hangs Over America," the newspapers report. Is the storm past, or has it just been postponed? Could it be this chronic bad weather? Who knows.

People are rioting in Kansas City, though.

April 10, 1968. We have arrived in Orlando, Florida, after an eleven-hour flight. The city lies calm underneath a summerlike sun; nothing here or at the New York airport, for that matter, suggests the fever gripping other American cities. We might as well be halfway around the world from them—on the Riviera, for example. My breakfast this morning was brought to me by a black, the first one I have ever been alone with in the same room. I tried to be as casual as possible in view of the fact that he was big enough to crush me like an ant, especially in my supine position.

Today I want to visit the streets and stores of Orlando and the auditorium where I will be singing. America seems to be emerging from its fever. Maybe the extremists are being calmed by the example of Mrs. Martin Luther King, who bears her grief with the same magnificent dignity that Jacqueline Kennedy showed when her husband was assassinated. Mrs. King continues to advocate nonviolence, even though she of all people has the right to revolt. She has vowed to continue the work of her husband. Ah, these Americans!

Wonderful weather in a wonderful place. The storms seem to be retreating on all fronts from the American horizon!

Yesterday I watched the annual Academy Awards ceremony on color television. I was glad to see Mike Nichols get an award for his marvelous film *The Graduate.*

I was less enthusiastic about the ceremony itself. At a time when the world, and America especially, is at such a tragic pass, this assembly of flamboyant people covered with jewels and furs seemed out of place and old-fashioned. The fact that most of the participants were no longer young helped to give the ceremony the air of an institution that had outlived its usefulness. Maybe there was something wrong with my color reception, but I distinctly saw the unlucky nominees go yellow when the winners were announced.

Conclusion: Hollywood society, the old show-business bulwark, is beginning to show its wigs and wrinkles. It is hard to take it seriously in 1968. Which reminds me, I had better not present myself for close public scrutiny, except when performing!

Pretty soon now, I am in for an award myself. Next week in New York I am to receive a "Tony," a special theater award, in recognition of my long career. The ceremony is to be televised, and after what I saw of the Academy Awards it behooves me to act simply and honestly in front of the camera. Not that I would act otherwise; I have always felt that sincerity was vital to my profession. And how could I *not* be sincere in my thanks to America!

Recently I saw *Guess Who's Coming to Dinner?* with Katharine Hepburn and Spencer Tracy, a dramatic presentation of the racial problem. Spencer Tracy finished this movie only a few weeks before his death. Katharine Hepburn got an Oscar for her role; I think he should have gotten one, posthumously, for his. Hollywood owed him this one last homage. And can you imagine the reaction when they announced a double Oscar to Spencer Tracy and the great love of his life? I am not saying that Rod Steiger did not deserve his Best Actor award; but he is only forty-three and will have plenty of other opportunities to land one. An example of Hollywood heartlessness? It would not be the first.

I am always worried when I have to pick up again where I left off. What if some part of my motor has rusted and refuses to operate at a crucial moment? Well, last night's concert, first of this new American tour, went contrary to all my worst expectations. I sang well, and the auditorium was fuller than I expected in this season of discontent. Only time will tell if America's troubles will hurt me at the box office. In the meantime my job is to go on giving people pleasure, and if I don't get caught in a racial battle, I will consider myself lucky all around. It is a time to be philosophical.

Miami is the favorite watering place for Big New Money. Its luxurious hotels are always filled to bursting with guests, and big-name attractions perform twice a night before an ever-changing sea of faces. So far no racial problems have come to ruffle Miami's indolent calm. The city is hot and humid and haunted by the noisy rich who can spent vast sums of money without blinking to "have a good time." It reminds me of Las Vegas, another city where Americans seek out their version of the Good Life. They are basically generous, nice people, these gaudy vacationers.

Tomorrow night I will be singing in Miami's Dade County Auditorium, a fine modern hall that I am told is sold out. Today will be taken up with interviews and putting on the smile.

Ça, c'est le show business.

Another great night, as openhearted and affectionate as a Walt Disney creation. Miami is as fabulous as ever. Many of its younger citizens were in the audience, and everybody looked so happy I felt like the world's most beneficial old man. I hope that I can always remain worthy of the confidence my audiences have in me, because it is they who have given me such a splendid old age.

On to St. Petersburg, Florida. What a curious name for such a progressive city! The beach is as long as the one at Ostende, on the North Sea, and the temperature as hot as the Riviera in August. The concert hall is wonderfully modern. But nothing, from my point of view, can rival the splendor of the "Sunken Gardens" through which I strolled today. This park is an orgy of blindingly beautiful flowers and the rarest kind of trees. If I had a spot like this at La Louque, you would find me there at least two hours a day, reading, writing and dreaming.

April 21, 1968. New York between two engagements to receive my "Tony" award. The presentation ceremony was well organized and more lively than I expected, with an enthusiastic audience of theater people. I was introduced by Audrey Hepburn, who had come over from Switzerland to receive a "Tony" of her own. My speech of thanks was short but 100 percent sincere, and all America could see it live on nationwide television. Afterward I was told that I had provided one of the high spots of the evening. The next morning I woke up a touch sad because I realized that the "Tony" ceremony was to be my last appearance on the New York stage.

Back to Washington, which seems to have returned to normal. Three more weeks of daily performances and I'll be home at La Louque. The time for my final retirement is drawing near. It will take all the wisdom and humility I possess to face it without self-pity.

We are staying at the Linden Hill Hotel on the outskirts of Washington where all is calm, green and practically deserted. I am going to spend a week at the Shady Grove Music Fair, the newest and most modern theater-in-the-round I have performed in so far. Tickets for my appearances have been selling slowly. Once again I am given the explanation that people in Washington are afraid to go out at night, even in their cars. I have chosen a difficult period. It appears that the "Tony" telecast provided some unexpected publicity for me, but until the results begin to show at the box office I will just have to be very humble and thank my lucky star that I am alive and alert.

Actually, my audience opening night was small but warm, and we got on very well. The next night, the audience was half again as large. Together we survived an incredibly humid evening in splendid good humor. I celebrated this turn for the better by eating out the following day in a Washington restaurant specializing in the food of Alsace. Not far from our table sat a couple that you would never have seen here till recently: a lovely young black girl with a distinguished-looking white. She came over to me with a shy but dazzling smile and asked me to autograph her menu. "My name is Sylvia," she added. I flashed her a great big integrationist grin and complied with her request. Her escort gave me a friendly wave of the hand and nobody involved seemed the slightest bit surprised.

After lunch we took a drive around the sections of Washington hardest hit during the riots. I was absolutely shocked by the extent of this senseless destruction.

My third performance was well attended. Washington

residents had been driven out to the theater in busses, except for the brave few who came in their cars. The management seemed delighted with the results, and finally I felt I was in control again.

We started off our fourth day with lunch in another of Washington's French restaurants. To our surprise, Mr. Sargent Shriver, just named Ambassador to France, came over to join us. I found him young, charming and as nervous as an adolescent about his diplomatic debut in front of General de Gaulle. None of us of course was qualified to help him, but we did suggest that his association with the Kennedy family would immediately place him high in the estimation of the French people. I added that I would do everything in my power as a representative of international show business to help him with his reception, and I would do it with pleasure because I consider America to be my second fatherland. A photographer came along and asked us to pose clinking glasses to Franco-American friendship. The next morning our picture was prominently placed in the Washington *Post*.

After lunch we took advantage of a special invitation to visit the White House. We did not see the inhabitants; that would have been too much to ask. A guide was there to lead us through the mansion and tell us of its history. We were all very excited at being inside a place that houses so many worries and so many momentous decisions.

Westbury, New York. Here everything seems calm despite the proximity to Harlem. Maybe troublemakers of both colors have been silenced by the wonderful example of Martin Luther King's widow.

A good piece of news: Paris has been chosen as the site for the first round of talks in the Vietnam peace negotiations. Perhaps this decision will relieve the growing tension between France and the United States.

Look magazine has just sent me the proofs for an article about me that will be appearing on the newsstands several days from now. We prepared this article two months ago at La Louque, and the results are gratifying. It's another feather in his cap for the old Paris street kid, because no other tribute to my age and my career will reach so many people.

New offers, new proposals keep coming in daily. I know I am right to stop while people are still asking for me and coming to say goodbye with tears in their eyes. Now when I want to talk to them I will do television shows from La Louque. That way I will reach millions of viewers and be even a better link between France and the world. And my love for my public will be all the more visible!

Back to Flint, Michigan, where I sang only a few months ago and was asked to return. I perform this evening. Two weeks from now I will have finished my farewells to American show business and I will be back at La Louque preparing for my Canadian and South American farewells. It is too early to start thinking about my Paris stint. For the moment I must content myself with the thought that I have just about made it.

I was nervous and tense during my Flint concert. I wonder why? No harm done; the audience was happy. Now I am in Chicago. Word is that the show is sold out; there will even be extra seats on the stage. But I don't feel very well and fear for my voice.

I have just been on television again, this time in a short film made during my stay in Orlando that was telecast at the very end of a news program. I assume it was seen all over America—always an impressive thought, though right now I am tired, nervous and not easily impressed. Old familiar feelings.

Chicago's Orchestra Hall is one of my favorite places in which to perform. Despite its vastness, it always seems rather intimate. Last night there must have been three thousand people in the audience, and I had a wonderful time with them. While I was up on stage receiving their accolades, all of a sudden I remembered the night of my stage debut at the age of twelve. The scene was the Café des Trois Lions, on the Boulevard de Ménilmontant. The people in the audience had paid twenty-five centimes for their drink and the entertainment. The show consisted of amateurs like me who were paid for their efforts with a drink at the bar. And now here I was, almost sixty-eight years later, sharing the stage of Orchestra Hall in Chicago with the ghosts of some of the world's greatest virtuosos. Take-off, arrival. In a way my presence on this stage meant that I had gained the same prominence in my line of work as Horowitz has in his.

In short, a show-business fairy tale.

France is in big trouble. A rebellion of French university students, later joined by the labor unions, has grown so fast and so big that the country is almost paralyzed. Air France is no longer landing at Orly or Le Bourget, the two Paris airports. When, after tomorrow night's concert in Detroit, we head back to La Louque, we will probably be rerouted via Brussels. There is no question of our not going; I am in far too big a hurry to get home!

Two cars were waiting for us at Brussels to drive us back to Marnes-la-Coquette. I have never seen France in such a turmoil. The General is going to speak to us on television; nobody knows his thoughts. What's up? I am at home, an impartial spectator, and, like everybody else in this country, glued to my television set.

The Latin Quarter in Paris has erupted. Student rebels with fire in their eyes want to destroy the old France to build the new. Pleas to stay calm, insults, demands are flying thick and fast. The view I get from television of what is happening in Paris is not very attractive; death and destruction seem to be hanging in the air. Even here, safe at La Louque, I feel like a broom straw about to be carried off by a cyclone. Only *le bon Dieu* can decide the fate of France now.

I don't know what to make of it. Three days later a student and worker rebellion is turning into a political revolution. My heart and brain are suffering from what I hear on the radio and see on television.

The people in the Paris streets are conducting themselves with great courage and style. Their anxiety has not made them forget how to laugh. As for me, I am proud to walk among these men and women, boys and girls, who represent my people and my country.

The situation is getting worse, not better. General de Gaulle looked tired and discouraged when he spoke on television the other day, and his speech only made the rebels flare up again. Now the unions are attacking the government even harder than before. I think there can now be no doubt that a revolution is in progress.

Pompidou is showing great energy in dealing with the situation, but the government as a whole no longer has its hand on the tiller. The country is drifting, and different factions are fighting among themselves to decide who will captain the boat. One thing is certain: France will never be the same again. We seem to be heading toward some new and as yet undefinable destiny, and all we can do is to hope it is not a tragic one.

Every day the Latin Quarter is the scene of marches organized in defiance of the forces of the law that are stationed there. These wild-eyed kids are staring death in the face. What is happening to the French? Have they been bitten by the same bug that caused the American university troubles of last year?

The foreign press, which follows all developments closely, is already predicting the fall of the government. It is obvious that our chaos is making other countries fear for their own order. Meanwhile, General de Gaulle has pulled a coup. He has spoken to the French people on television with new strength and firmness. Even though his voice was cracking with emotion, he seemed to be again the General de Gaulle of old. And now the radio, our faithful companion in this crazy period, is keeping us informed of the General's attempts to regain lost ground.

The miracle has happened. France is calm once more, and some of de Gaulle's adversaries seem to be backing down on their demands. Perhaps revolution is not inevitable after all. In certain industries people are even going back to work. Is this a maneuver on their part, or have they finally seen the light?

In any event, good weather and gasoline are back. The crowds on the streets and boulevards look relieved and happy. And when an enormous group of government sympathizers decided to march up the Champs-Élysées from the Place de la Concorde to the Arc de Triomphe, there were no adverse reactions. Nobody came to attack this orderly procession of people who refuse to see France fall victim to anarchy.

Now we hear that most workers are scheduled to be back at their jobs at the beginning of next week. It is now June 2. We have seen France tremble and grow weaker, as if just about to perish, and then rise from its deathbed to walk again. It is too soon to announce that the patient has recovered. There has been one show of force in the streets; there can always be another.

One thing is sure: People in France are glad to be less afraid for a while. Over Pentecost weekend they left Paris in droves, thanks to the miraculous return of gasoline.

The parks around the city were covered with families who had come to stretch their legs and breathe freely again. Meanwhile, on the boulevards, up and down the Champs-Élysées, the crowds are gay—in a sort of nervous fashion.

We hoped. We prayed. To no avail.

The news hit the world with the force of an atomic bomb. After John Kennedy, after Martin Luther King, Robert Kennedy is dead from an assassin's bullet. Another of America's great hopes is dashed forever.

We were watching him from Los Angeles on television. He was smiling the young and gentle smile that almost made people forget how tough and determined he was inside. Then all of a sudden he was on the ground, mortally wounded, with a crowd of supporters moaning and shrieking around him. He had fallen victim to the violence that is afflicting the entire world, even our gentle France.

Robert Kennedy had come to see me in my dressing room at Constitution Hall in Washington during one of my earlier tours. He was with my friends Monsieur Hervé Alphand, the French Ambassador, and his wife. John Kennedy was still President at that time, and the apple of everybody's eye. I told Bob that his brother's example was going to bring young politicos to the fore all over the world. Bob smiled without answering, and held out his hand.

Afterward I had the good fortune to meet him several times in New York. One night we found ourselves eating in the same restaurant. Bob got up from his table and came over to thank me gravely for my unwavering admiration for the extraordinary Kennedy clan.

Oh, what is happening to the America I love, the America I remember so fondly? And what will happen to Paris, the city of smiles, now that it has become the troublemaker for all of France? Will it ever be itself again?

It is June 16. Elections are in the offing. The country is feeling better, but it is still a little unsteady on its pins. Let's hope there will be no relapses.

Unlike many other show-business people, I said nothing during the events of May. Not that I am criticizing those who did; it is just that I have no bones to pick. I feel grateful to all the Frenchmen who come to see me regardless of their politics, just as I feel grateful to all my audiences all over the world. They have made it possible for me to live as I do and look after my loved ones. They have given my reputation its luster. I love them all and I have no reason to take exception to anyone anywhere. And what's more, I think that at my age I have the right to look at things my way.

Good luck, France. You are now part of the new world where the young often fly in the face of their elders, parents and relations included, and inform them that it is an indignity to be over thirty.

I am busy preparing my one-man show in French for North and South America and Spain. Would you please excuse me while I rehearse some songs?

July 24, 1968. We're off, and we won't be back until September, the month of my eightieth birthday.

In France, the lessons of the May events seem to have been digested. The voters of France have opted for the same government but new priorities.

I am very pleased with my French material. Of course, my opinion doesn't count for everything. The final judgment is made by the audience, in this case the opening-night public in São Paulo. I've been behaving myself; I'm at the top of my form. Now let's see what the public thinks.

Coming in for a landing over Rio de Janeiro at night, we had a magnificent view of the lights of the bay that forms a kind of antechamber to the city.

I am told that everything is ready for tomorrow's performance in São Paulo. Today I spent with members of the press in Rio, who were kind and affectionate. They had a lot of questions to ask me about recent events in France. What did I think of Cohn-Bendit, the young student agitator? I don't know him, I answered, and so I can't have any opinion. What was my feeling about the rebellion of the students in the Latin Quarter? Well, I said, the whole world is feverish, and it is normal for kids to suffer from higher temperatures than adults. Would I have followed Alain Delon's example during the theater strike and gone on playing? I don't know, I'm not Delon. But did I approve of his actions? I approve of anyone who has the courage to do what he thinks is right.

And so forth and so on until I had finally made it clear that I had come to Brazil to sing and not to add fuel to the fire of international controversies. One last question: What did I think about censorship? Never had any problem with it, I said, even for certain unmentionable mentions I may have made in my songs.

So much for Brazil's impressions of me. As for my impressions of Brazil, there seemed to be a lot of uneasiness. The Brazilians are as always simple, pleasant and direct; but the people in the streets seem to have lost their sunniness, and the upper classes no longer look as elegant and robust. But isn't this kind of change related to what is happening all over the world? Everywhere my Eightieth Birthday Tour has taken me, including my own country, I have noticed the same fatalism. I am beginning, just beginning, to be eager to go into retreat. I have been out proving myself long enough. But certainly I am not the only person who is reluctant to retire. Look at all the heads of state whose ambition has not been diminished in the slightest by all the worries of their office. It is the impetus that takes you to the top that makes you want to keep on going. And so, like those old Ménilmontant draft horses, you keep on going.

The first performance in São Paulo took place in front of a television stage set because the local broadcasting station wanted to film it for later use. The combination of the shimmering decor and the new material I was introducing made me very jittery, and the two hours I spent on stage seemed like years.

The second night's performance completely cured me of my ailments. The audience was wonderful; many of the people came for a second time. I swung into my new songs with more confidence and was happy to feel the momentum that they gave to my show. It is a better show than some of my older ones, more in tune with the times, more simple and direct. The fact that there is nothing aggressive or pushy about it means that I can soft-pedal most of the time and save the punch for critical moments. This is my favorite technique. It means that I can keep my audience happy for two hours without using up my energies and then really let them have it when the time is ripe.

Simple? Simple.

I leave for Rio confident that my new show in French is ready for public consumption. Somebody last night told me I was the biggest thing ever to hit Brazil. I'm in seventh heaven!

I have sung in Rio's Municipal Theater once before, five years ago. I remember the occasion with pleasure. This time the ticket sales from the opening night were to benefit Brazilian polio victims. Seats were very expensive, and my audience was rich and blasé. I had to work to warm them up, but as soon as I had them on my side, they decided to stay with me till the end.

I continue to work over the details of my show like a fussy old craftsman.

The television cameras were grinding away again for my second performance in Rio. Again, three standing ovations to be captured on film. I feel better each time I enter stage left. For one thing, I know that this is the last big effort; and then, every show I do makes me more confident of my program. My voice and my nerves are holding out. I am getting across to my audience. One more city in Brazil, Porto Alegre, then Buenos Aires. And then, and then, and then . . .

Boy, am I ever going to pamper myself when my Eightieth Birthday Tour is over!

But it not over yet. Porto Alegre is waiting, another São Paulo growing by leaps and bounds. The people are as gay as the name of their city suggests.

As always in Brazil, the first thing I did when I got here was to find the city's botanical garden and take a solitary walk to sort things out in my head. Surrounded by old trees, rare plants and gorgeous flowers, I find the energy to urge myself on. Why am I so conscientious? Why can't I allow myself some lapses, like the rest of the human race?

I think perfectionism has become a game for me, as well as a requirement.

August 5, 1968. Porto Alegre and I had our rendezvous in a big municipal hall. Once again the television cameras were present; the films they are taking can be used only once in the three months following my performance, and only on the closed television circuit within the city. The fact that only a few of the people there understood

French did not seem to dampen the enthusiasm of my audience.

I have a head cold, or at least I hope that's what it is. We are leaving for Buenos Aires.

What a reception! I feel like a visiting prince. People came up to me in my hotel to thank me for honoring their city with my visit—when it is I who should be thanking them for making so much of me. I am at the top of my form, and during my six-day stand on the stage of their opera house I intend to sing my heart out.

I still pray, just in case, but I feel protected. My cold for some reason seems to have loosened my vocal cords instead of reducing them to silence. I have my profession, my public, my record, and a sense of devotion to all of them. In return they give me pride and joy. Why am I so favored at a time when people are destroying each other and losing all faith? Why have I been guided by some divine hand toward the joys of work and love and faithful friendship?

There is not much more I can ask of a life that has already been so good to me.

Opening night in Buenos Aires was a benefit for Argentinian polio victims. The public was as glossy as in Rio de Janeiro and had the same reaction. According to Argentinian custom, the show was scheduled for ten-thirty at night, and I feel rather sleepy this morning. But the press is happy, and so am I. I have somehow prevailed over my own old age and the international political situation that has affected show business everywhere, but I have no time to congratulate myself for my good fortune. The important thing from now on will be—the performance. That's the acid test. Otherwise I will just try to keep mentally and physically fit so that this fall can find me celebrating my eightieth birthday on the Paris stage.

Our French heart-transplant case, Father Boulogne, has sent me a reply to the letter I wrote before leaving home. His neat handwriting and monastic style have not changed a bit since he received another person's heart. What an eerie thought! I still feel like going to see the greatest surgeon in France when I get back and having him give me the liver, the gall bladder and the brain of a saint, and, while he is at it, the saint's you-know-what too. That way my thoughts will forever after be nothing but pure.

I have spent my last evening as a performer in Buenos Aires. I won't ever forget these concerts and especially the happiness of the people who came to them; and they, I hope, will remember the old trouper who put them in such a state. Goodbye, Buenos Aires, so dear to my heart. Tomorrow we leave for Montevideo, where the students are up in arms. I go as a missionary, to sing them a song of hope.

This will be the beginning of the second half of the very last round of all. La Louque beckons. Soon I must step down; otherwise I will have used up all the stocks of energy I will need for my waning years. The old age I have in mind will demand a lot of energy. I want it to be good and gay, proud and philosophical, and it will be none of those things if I don't learn to slow down.

The lovely old theater where I performed last night in Montevideo, Uruguay, is a smaller version of La Scala in Milan, with four tiers of balconies divided into individual boxes. This time it was filled with a dressy public that really knew its French.

Eleven more concerts. My old goal, the Ultimate Performance, heaves into sight. When my carcass rebels, I tell it, "Soon I will be passing on the torch and settling down to be 'The Wise Man of Ménilmuche.'" That's my next goal and the final one.

Meanwhile, Santiago de Chile awaits me for two concerts. *Giddyap, dobbin.*

Santiago de Chile: Assaulted at the airport. Flashbulbs, photographers, projectors, television cameras, reporters, microphones thrust under my nose, a thousand questions.

I had the feeling that I was saying absolute nonsense, but went on saying it anyway.

Last night's audience was charming and reacted right off the bat to the program in French. Many of the people there were members of French families living in Chile for various reasons, and many of them were moved to tears by the bit of France I brought them.

I am on the front page of all the Santiago newspapers. This Eightieth Birthday Tour is a first, a show-business record. I swear to heaven that I have never worked harder. And when the old nag doesn't want to go any farther? It advances anyway, because it wants me to enjoy this final victory.

I had lunch with the French Ambassador to Chile, who attended the concert last night. This evening's concert took place in an indoor sports arena, with a stage set up in the middle, and close to four thousand spectators. Because most of them understood French, I got up some real momentum. Looking at them afterward, I thought that Chileans must surely have the biggest, softest eyes in the world.

Nine more concerts to go!

I have just had a terribly disturbing piece of news: Dwight Eisenhower is dying in Washington. He and Walt Disney were my great heroes. The Lady in Black never lets up, does she?

August 22, 1968. Last night's audience in the Municipal Theater in Lima was elegant and easy to please. The hall was filled to the rafters with fans plus the ever-present television cameramen. My only worry was my voice—uncertain, I felt. This morning I woke up with a persistent frog in my throat. Understandable. At my age, I can still take the performing but not the frills: the photographers, the favor-seekers, the autograph hounds, the trips.

Well, that's better. My voice has returned. I had no trouble at all with it at last night's concert in the ballroom of the Hotel Crillon in Lima, a benefit for the Peruvian cancer society.

By the way, it appears I have a half-sister, on my father's side, living in an old-age institution here in Lima. Her name, she says, is Rose Chevalier, and she is eighty-two years of age. I have asked her to produce some proof of her origins before I will think of going to meet her. There is something very fishy about this relative I have been unaware of for going on eighty years. And now I am told that there are two more old parties in Mexico City waiting to hold me in a sisterly embrace. Goodness, Papa, you really spread yourself thin!

We arrived in Panama at two-thirty in the morning. I nearly fainted when one of my managers, there at the airport to meet me, informed me that a group of French people were giving a party for me and hoped I would come over right away. "Now?" I asked. "Oh, it's not far," he answered. By then it was three-thirty in the morning, so I thanked him kindly and said that I would really like to get a few hours' sleep before being introduced to these eager new friends. Some people do not seem to realize that when you are my age you do not go out on the town at any hour of the day or night.

Today we took a drive through the side streets and poorer neighborhoods of the oldest part of Panama City, where a colorful people live out their clean and busy lives. Then we went to the newer residential sections, green and lovely, and to the finest lookouts over de Lesseps' famous canal. So much for the French influence in Panama; Spain obviously inspired the smaller dwellings, and the larger apartment buildings are in the American style. The result is an unexpected corner of this modern world where French, American and Spanish influences coexist in harmony and where life seems simpler and sweeter than elsewhere.

I suspect I will have to give a bilingual concert. . . .

I was right. Only a small number of people in last night's audience could understand French. I quickly switched back to my English-French program, and from that time on everything was rosy.

Which is not to say it wasn't a real acrobatic feat. During my entire South American tour I had been perfecting my new French material for the acid test of my Paris appearances. In so doing, I had let my English material fall by the wayside. And now here I was, suddenly obliged to produce it from nowhere.

My memory did not fail me for an instant, and neither did my nerves. It is at times like these that a performer has to call upon his true stuff.

More thoughts about my retirement. How will I adjust to this new kind of life? Never stepping on stage again. Never being gripped again by stage fright about four in the afternoon just at the thought of the evening's performance. Never going to bed again after the show, proud and relieved to have survived and succeeded.

I have never known another kind of life. Will I be lost without it? Or will I be calmer, more philosophical? My capacity for serene resignation is really going to be put to the test this time, by the biggest sacrifice of all. I have always enjoyed such independence as a person and as a performer. Only I was responsible for my work, my reputation and my services to my country. And now only I can answer for my decision to step down.

Will I still have the same freedom?

Courage, Momo. You are getting out while the getting is good, while you are still winning and can take a dignified bow. Refusing to stop after your eightieth birthday would be going too far. Too far: those are the key words. Everything has an end, and it should be on the near side of far.

More fanfare greeted me on arrival at Mexico City. Flashbulbs, television cameras, ten reporters talking all at once—the usual business. I had to inch my way down the gangplank to the room where I was to meet the Mexican press. And when I arrived at my hotel, I found an orchestra and singers waiting to receive me, in a tribute from this lively and progressive city.

The next day I went to a reception given in the headquarters of a French cultural organization. The guests ranged from the French Ambassador to Mexico to an old army pal from my World War I regiment whom I had not seen since 1914. Not to mention all the French living in Mexico, the Mexicans who spoke French, and, as always, reporters and photographers. There were so many people that my feet scarcely touched ground.

The reception ended with a press conference held in a small side room. I was asked questions of all kinds:

Q: How do you stay so young and healthy-looking?

A: Because I'm mentally uncomplicated. (Laughter.)

Q: How does the symbol of French wit and grace feel about women?

A: The body of a pretty girl is our Creator's finest work.

Q: What do you think of international student movements?

A: I left school when I was eleven. I never resumed my studies, and I never was a student. Under these circumstances it is difficult for me to form an opinion. Anyway, at home and abroad, I don't mix with politics. My job is to make people forget that politics exist!

And so forth and so on.

The first of my two gala performances in Mexico City was the biggest triumph so far. Extra chairs had to be put on the stage to hold all the people, and the audience reacted quickly to everything I said or sang in French. Evenings like these are a performer's greatest joy, especially when he's the kind who puts his profession and his public before anything else. Because the reception the audience has in store for you makes all the sacrifices seem worthwhile.

Today I had lunch at the French Ambassador's handsome and inviting house. Madame Vimont, the Ambassador's wife, placed me to her right at table, which made me the guest of honor among all these distinguished people!

My sympathies really lie with the common people, my own people of the streets. But I owe such a huge debt of gratitude to all the others, to everyone, that rich and poor, powerful and modest live together in my heart.

September 2, 1968. Summer vacations are over, and in the Mexico City and New York airports chaos reigns. A traveler has no choice but to stand pat and stay calm and abandon any thoughts he has of salvaging his dignity. Finally we reached Montreal, where we had one night to recuperate before leaving for Quebec.

It has been five years since I have seen Quebec. Looking out the window as we drove from the airport to the

Château Frontenac Hotel, I could see that the citizens of the city had not been sitting on their hands in my absence. Quebec is even gayer and more seductive than before and certainly more modern. The new houses, office buildings, hospitals and medical school radiate a wonderful good health.

Today I do the first of my two shows in the pretty theater in the Palais Montcalm. It appears that Quebec's students are threatening rebellion also. Hmmm. Rebellion is not good for my box office. The fact of the matter is, there is not a corner of the world where you can go to escape trouble, and if you are trying to stay neutral, like me, the best you can do is to stand firmly on your record and the quality of your work. This is the best defense you have.

The good Lord willing, in five days I will be home. I set out on this tour before the world situation really became serious, and I will return before it explodes. I've been lucky. If the prophets of doom are right, this autumn ought to be turbulent, and I will already be home safe at La Louque.

My favorite author is Montaigne, the great French writer of the sixteenth century. Montaigne avoided getting involved in politics by saying that he had confidence in the chosen leaders of the country. Then he retired to the provinces to concentrate on his writing. What was good for him is good enough for me. He wrote about life: that is all I sing about. For the rest of my life his example will suffice.

After two rewarding nights in Quebec, we are now in Montreal, where I will perform this evening to a full house in the big, modern theater of the Palais des Arts. My friend Roger Champoux, editor-in-chief of the Canadian newspaper *La Presse*, gave a cocktail party for me today where I met some of Montreal's most distinguished citizens, including the mayor, Monsieur Drapeau. This is the last stop on my last trip to the Americas as a performer.

The return to Paris was a kind of happy nightmare. French television had organized entire programs in my honor. The Musée de la Chanson (Museum of Song) presented an exhibition covering my sixty-eight years as a performer. And on the big day itself, September 12, 1968, everybody who was anybody in Paris show business was invited to the Lido for a birthday party. The foreign stars who happened to be in Paris were on the guest list, too. After the show at the Lido, we were all treated to a short film recalling the highlights of my career. An up-and-coming young comedian, Jean Yanne, gave a speech about me that was tongue-in-cheek but also full of affection. At the end I came up on stage to salute all my Parisian friends and thank them from the bottom of my heart for their sentimental tribute.

At dinner I sat between Noel Coward on my left, and on my right, Claudette Colbert, as beautiful as ever; Claudette had been my co-star in *The Smiling Lieutenant*, filmed on Long Island in 1932, under Ernst Lubitsch's direction.

And then, as if this excitement were not enough for my old nerves, there were the interviews in which I spent whole days recounting my life, visits from newsmen, photographers, and radio and television reporters. I nearly dropped from exhaustion. I also talked too much. Silly questions, silly answers. When you have to say the same things many times a day you begin to be embarrassed by your own inanity.

I can hear you saying that I have no right to complain. That is true. But an old man can reach a point where too much happiness is bad for him. I knew very well while all this was going on that I had two test runs still to do, one in Madrid and another in Palma de Mallorca, before I would show my new material on the Champs-Élysées.

The most touching item at the exhibition organized by the Musée de la Chanson is a photograph of Fréhel. The singer was about twenty years old in this picture, which must have been taken in 1907, about the time when I was first hearing love's call. My goodness, she was beautiful. It is easy to see why I leapt when she beckoned. Her body was as beautiful as her face, but already the devil was in her. He got to work on me as well and made me take in too much alcohol, too many drugs when I was with her. Our relationship lasted until my career began to suffer, and then I left her, my heart bleeding. There was no question of my staying near a woman who could totally destroy me, but I certainly took a long time to recover from her.

Friends who have been to this exhibition swear that

even in this photograph they detect a glimmer of madness in her eyes. For Fréhel was soon to ruin her talent and beauty with a senselessly destructive personal life. Only a few years after this photograph was taken she had completely lost her luster. Then she left for Roumania, probably in the company of a lover, and when she returned to France her looks were gone forever and her character was deformed. But she managed to hold onto the dregs of her talent until her unfortunate death.

With a little intelligence and love, she might have been one of the great vocalists of our era. She never forgave me for abandoning her to her fate.

At my age, you look back on early passions like these with a certain tenderness. If you ever have the occasion to meet a former flame again, one of two things happens. Either you express your gratitude for wonderful moments spent together, or you are overwhelmed by the memory of the venom at the end. Since I was not made for being aggressive, those are the encounters I dread most.

Madrid treated me with the tender affection I have learned to expect there, but Palma de Mallorca was the big surprise. I have heard about Palma many times, of course, but I had never been there before and nothing had prepared me for its beauty. Here is a seaside resort that combines in a single spot all the charms of our entire Riviera. Sometimes you think you are in St. Tropez, then in Cannes or Juan-les-Pins. And all day long the sea lies before you blue and inviting. At night I fell asleep like a baby listening to the lapping of the waves and woke up refreshed in the morning. I even found it possible to imagine performing on the Champs-Élysées three days hence, in full possession of my capacities, but I knocked on wood just to make sure.

Palma de Mallorca provided me with a cosmopolitan audience, and we got along famously. I slept for a few hours after the performance, spent another hour in a state of semi-wakefulness and finally dragged myself to the airport for an early plane to Paris. I came straight home, kissed my La Louque household and fell back into bed.

My nerves were jangling. It was impossible to sleep, and I had to sleep. My Paris opening was only two days away. I took a sleeping pill, supposedly mild, and went out like a light almost the moment I swallowed it. As I slipped back into consciousness again, some hours later, I thought I saw the Lady in Black gliding toward me. She was looking at me with maternal compassion. "Soon you can sleep like that forever, my little one," her eyes seemed to say. And I lay there, calm and smiling, while she came in my direction. Brrrrrrrrr.

This evening I face a houseful of hardened Paris first-nighters for the grand opening of my series of nineteen farewell recitals. To the slaughterhouse.

Slaughterhouse?

Never have I known a reception like the one last night. Glossy Paris, decked out in all its finery, rose to its feet.

The greatest names in Paris—the Begum Aga Khan, Monsieur and Madame Hervé Alphand, Monsieur Louis Armand, Marcel Pagnol and more—stood and cheered for five minutes straight when I made my entrance on stage. Yup, before I said a word.

I started talking to myself: *Steady, boy, you must not cry, think of your modest dignity, there, there now . . .* My breath started to come in little jerks. My voice thickened several times with emotion. I could have killed myself right then and there for love.

Then at the end—you guessed it—the whole house was on its feet again, this time for ten minutes, cheering and waving its arms. In my dressing room afterward I was overwhelmed by a crowd of celebrities hugging and kissing me while I perspired profusely. Never have I seen anything like it. For anyone. Anywhere.

This morning's press was unanimous in its enthusiasm, not a dissenter, not a single sour word.

The most blasé, the most steely-eyed Parisians had come to the Théâtre des Champs-Élysées to see me and had shown themselves to be openhearted, enthusiastic, miraculously human people.

It was the same story for each of the performances during the three weeks that followed. Together my public and the critics decided that it was too early for me to retire, that I should return next year, that my show had never been more simple, more perfect.

One thought after another tumbled in my tired old head. To leave? Or not to leave?

At the end of the last performance, the answer surfaced from somewhere deep in my subconscious. I heard myself announcing to my audience that of the sixty cities I had sung to during the course of my eightieth year, Paris was the one that had treated me with the greatest affection and love, and I saw no reason to aim any higher. The moment had come to abandon stage and recitals.

And the moment was well chosen. Offers were still pouring in, but I knew, in my heart of hearts, that I could not go on much longer without faltering.

I was leaving a career that had been, for sixty-eight years, my livelihood and my reason for living.

Nothing could make me tarnish that record.

Part Two

A New Life, New Hope

Here I am—my new life awaits me. Last night I said my adieux to the stage—and how do I feel this morning?

Mostly I feel relieved. How nice to have nothing urgent to do! That's a weight off my mind already.

We drank champagne at La Louque last night. The Paquets were there and I asked Janie Michels to come over; I needed some feminine sympathy. It was a good idea to say those farewells, but the whole thing hasn't been easy. When I went up to bed I was still full of courage—and wine, and feeling somewhat dazed. I spent a restless night.

This morning I read the notices in the newspapers; they were all enthusiastic. Olivier Merlin wrote a moving article in *Le Monde*, and the *Herald Tribune* gave a good summary of my farewell speech and called me a master showman. There was also a packet of letters from friends who had seen my last performance.

This afternoon for the first time in ages I went to see a movie: *Phèdre,* with Marie Bell. What a wonderful actress she is! People like her—strong and talented people whom I've always admired—seem less remote to me now.

Their quality always prevails, and this film proves it. From now on there will be no more doubts about Marie Bell's gifts as a tragic actress. And she got this role when she needed it most, while struggling with ill health. Marvelous Marie Bell. What a long way she has come! I remember when she was just another shapely young thing at the Comédie Française, and now she's one of the greats. She has joined the ranks of actresses like Sarah Bernhardt and now Elvire Popesco who have fought off sickness, age and even death with sheer guts and inner fire. I think that fate is kinder to those who have given their all to an art or a profession. They are our inspiration and our guide, the glory of the theater.

The second day of my new life: Saw *Romeo and Juliet* at the five-o'clock showing at the Paramount Élysées. The director of the film, Franco Zeffirelli, has cooked up a dazzling feast in which the sauce rather drowns the goose. *Phèdre* is more to my liking.

I had a whiskey over dinner tonight and made another tipsy exit. I mustn't start drinking again. If I had any doubts about leaving the stage, I could use that as an excuse to drink. But I don't. An old actor can go on indefinitely: he can get up there on the stage from time to time, if he's still steady on his pins and can remember his lines. An old musician, too. He can even sit down while we listen to him serve up the art of the great composers.

But an old boulevardier is something else again. It doesn't take much to make him seem indecent. He has to stand. He's all alone, with no works of genius to rely on.

He sings and romps around for two hours straight, the length of his performance. *Non et non!* That's not for me now. But this does not mean my life is over. I have not cut it short, and I shall go on.

I just saw *The Thomas Crown Affair.* Norman Jewison, the director, has made enormous progress. He has directed his two stars, Faye Dunaway and Steve McQueen, with such sobriety and skill that you want to hug them at the end. He will be one of Hollywood's greatest directors, and the competition out there is pretty stiff. I am proud of having worked with him for American television. That was a few years ago, and I can still remember how easy it was to follow his good advice.

Last night at the King Club, a chic restaurant of Saint-Germain-des-Prés, Charles Aznavour wined and dined twenty friends, all of them great stars of the Sixties. Ambassador Shriver and his wife came for drinks beforehand, and at dinner I was seated between Michèle Morgan and a lovely young star named France Anglade. Everything was festive and gay and everyone professionally fraternal. Each guest seemed to bring out the best in all the others. I chatted with Michèle Morgan about the somewhat similar ways we've passed from youth to . . . well, the aftermath, and with France Anglade about her recent rise to stardom. All in all, it was an enjoyable excursion into a part of Paris that has come to symbolize all that is new and young and beautiful.

I've reached an understanding with myself that deepens every day. I refuse all offers amicably, assuring people that my decision is quite firm. And I don't feel any regrets because I know I'm acting lucidly.

At my age you don't go on performing and courting disaster unless you need the money.

The Jacqueline Kennedy Onassis marriage shocked the world, but it has already found its champions, many famous writers among them. The outcry will certainly die down soon, as it should. As James de Coquet said in *Le Figaro,* "There's nothing scandalous about her preferring the caresses of fortune to the pitfalls of public widowhood." All of my best wishes are with this extraordinary and beautiful bride. I sent her this wire: ALL THE HAPPINESS IN THE WORLD MAGNIFICENT JACQUELINE STOP WISH MY NAME WERE ARISTOTLE ONASSIS INSTEAD OF MAURICE CHEVALIER.

The second week of my new life: I have lived with the decision and am getting used to it.

Maurice Chevalier's home just outside of Paris, called La Louque after his mother's tender nickname.

President Eisenhower comes to greet him at the Waldorf Astoria in New York.

Maurice Chevalier feeling a bit Texan, for no particular reason.

Maurice Chevalier chats with President Harry Truman in his home in Independence, Missouri.

Jacqueline Kennedy congratulates Maurice Chevalier after a performance at the Alvin Theater in New York.

Audrey Hepburn presents Maurice Chevalier with the Special Tony Award for distinguished service in the theater, in April 1968. The ceremony was his last appearance on the New York stage. *(Wide World photo)*

Chevalier with his American "Daddy" (so called because he is six days older!), "Mr. San Francisco" Louis R. Lurie, celebrating their birthdays at the San Francisco Hilton.

Maurice Chevalier and Sophie Tucker sing "I Remember It Well," from the film *Gigi*, on the Ed Sullivan Show.

Maurice Chevalier receives eightieth birthday congratulations from his good friend Senator Charles H. Percy in Washington.

Maurice Chevalier and American Ambassador Sargent Shriver toast French-American friendship in Paris.

Maurice Chevalier in a corner of his French home, which is filled

with works of art and mementos of his long and fulfilling career.

Maurice Chevalier presents his straw hat to Duke Ellington for the Jazz King's seventieth birthday in Paris.

The old Maurice is proud of the young Maurice.

Maurice Chevalier escorts Barbra Streisand to the premiere of *Funny Girl* at L'Opéra in Paris.

Maurice Chevalier appears on TV in Paris with Diahann Carroll, directed by J. C. Averty.

Maurice Chevalier congratulates astronaut Frank Borman, who is accompanied by his wife, right, and Mrs. Eunice Kennedy Shriver. (*Le Figaro photo*)

Maurice Chevalier with the sculpture of his mother, La Louque, a favorite spot in the garden of his home named for her near Paris.

Maurice Chevalier—reader, thinker, philosopher, new young writer with hopes—at home.

Maurice Chevalier walking in the garden of his French home, La Louque.

But recent events have left me in a state of intoxication. I find myself seeking distractions—like seeing old friends, accepting invitations to fancy dinner parties. The industrialist Paul-Louis Weiller has invited me to dine with the Windsors: I accepted with pride and pleasure! (*Listen, old boy, don't start getting snobbish; you haven't got the energy. You're riled up these days, but your last few grains of sense will prevail, I'm sure, in the end.*) Meanwhile Suzy Volterra invited me to join her at Longchamp for the closing of the racing season. Henri Bonnet, ex-Ambassador to Washington, Madame Derval, Robert Manuel and his beautiful Claudine, the Paquets and I made up a table with a charming view of the race track, the pride of Parisian bettors. We were so gay we almost caused a scandal; the slightest remark and we were off in gales of laughter. Champagne made everything even more festive. I put my money on only the great jockey Yves Saint-Martin and pretended to have won a fortune. The truth is my take amounted to two ten-franc bills and one fiver, which I pocketed with all the dignity I could muster.

La vie était belle.

The days are going by pleasantly enough, though I'm still worried about my future.

It was my own decision to leave the stage after my Paris triumph. But that may not stop people from thinking that I've had it, that I'm too old to be starting new projects. Not a surprising reaction considering that I'm going on eighty-one.

And what if they were right? I'd just have to face facts

and turn to philosophy as a last hope. I could still take pride in my career, of course; and nobody would see me disgrace myself and end up without a friend to my name. Yes, it would have been a lot worse if I'd gone on and spoiled my exit, like a lot of people I've seen. That really would have made me miserable.

When you're eighty you don't go chasing after anybody or anything anymore. Things must happen by themselves; other people must make the first move. If they don't, you shrug your shoulders. "*Au revoir*," you think, "see you on the moon." You don't push any more. If people need you, they seek you out, and if they ignore you, you ignore them. The sacrifice comes naturally.

Every day I feel farther from the world of music halls and recitals. I went as far as one can go in a great profession and I gave it everything I had. I've done my bit for the red, white and blue, and I'm not going to do any more. It is true that I understand my new goals less well than I understood the ones I lived with for so long and have just abandoned, but I move forward in the belief that I have chosen honestly and clearly.

I've gotten so much encouragement recently from writers I admire that I've decided to read more of their books. From now on I'll spend three hours a day on three different authors. For example, Elsa Triolet's *Ecoutez-*

voir in the morning, then some Félicien Marceau, and Marcel Pagnol at bedtime.

I'm at peace with myself. A flame lights my heart and mind, and I'm full of joy and hope. *Relax, friend; la vie est belle.*

Charles Munch just died at seventy during an American tour. He fell on the field of honor, practically right on the podium. He took his bows and lay down for a rest from which he'll never awaken. He was a fine old man, handsome as he was kind, unassuming as he was great, and he departed this world in a most enviable fashion. And he deserved to. It is almost as if he had gotten special dispensation and been lifted up by the Creator's hand so that he wouldn't suffer.

Gisèle d'Assailly Julliard, wife of the late publisher, gave a luncheon in my honor yesterday in her sumptuous apartment on the Rue de l'Université. Her brief but moving opening remarks gave me needed encouragement, and I responded with a toast to the memory of her husband, René Julliard, who was almost entirely responsible for the new direction my life has taken and for the pleasure I now get from writing.

Since I left the stage I've been indulging myself a bit in the champagne, whiskey, and wine department—such an easy habit to pick up again. It's so pleasant when it goes down well! But let's face it, I'm too vulnerable. I'll have to give it up completely. Half a glass of champagne and I stagger—all because of Menière's disease, an affliction of the inner ear that paid me the honor of a visit a few years back. I guess I'd better not forget it.

And coffee will have to defer to Sanka. Thanks to a reasonable dose of champagne and a less reasonable dose of coffee—two cups to be exact—imbibed at Gisèle's luncheon, combined with my excitement over my new life, I didn't sleep a wink last night. Just lay there wide awake, consoling myself with the thought that it was a lot less serious to suffer from insomnia than from poor Charles Munch's endless sleep. You have to learn to look at things in the best light.

La Facture (The Bill), Paris' latest hit play, marks the second success for its author, Françoise Dorin, and also for Jacqueline Maillan, a perfectly irresistible actress. The plot revolves around the idea that you pay for everything in life sooner or later; hence the title.

It's true, life thinks up lots of different "bills" and has some unbelievable ways of presenting them for payment. While I was sitting there amid all that welcome laughter, a feeling of anxiety began to come over me. It was much less welcome and indicative of my general state of mind as 1968 draws to a close. I suppose I'm really thinking of the inevitable "bill of health" that will fall due shortly. It's going to tell me which of my few remaining artistic hopes I'll have to give up forever and which ones I can still cling to. The noble virtue of sacrifice becomes a necessity when you're my age and the bill of health starts making its cruel demands.

Saw Françoise Sagan's movie *La Chamade.* I was delighted with certain parts of this story sketched in rather sordid halftones. Catherine Deneuve moved me throughout. If I were fifty years younger I'd be madly in love with her. They'd call her a beauty in any day and age. She's timeless. And adorable.

I have pangs—not very serious ones—at the idea that I can no longer count on the warmth of a receptive audience to take fifty years off my life at the end of each performance. From now on only my own flame can keep me lit. Or half lit. Or extinguished.

For the time being I continue to accept invitations to dinner when I want to keep in touch with whoever invited me. I went to a royal dinner at Paul-Louis Weiller's townhouse on the Rue de la Faisanderie. He had assembled fifty notables, from the Windsors to Salvador Dali. Sat at the Duchess's right at the table of honor, the attractive Princesse de Polignac at *my* right: pardon me while I drop a few names. *Merci.*

The Duchess is amazingly lively and funny. Philosophical too. One of the things she said to me was "When you go out and look bored, the result is that you bore everybody else too." As for the Duke, despite his ailing eye he keeps his good humor, his inner strength, his energetic kindness. Salvador Dali has added two bushy sideburns to the famous pointed mustache. Maurice Genevoix told me he's been my fan since the age of eighteen. I was grateful to Paul-Louis to have been so well treated and so amicably received by all this distinguished company. *Onward and upward, Momo of Ménilmuche!*

Had drinks with Professor and Madame Vallery-Radot on the Avenue Gabriel. I felt decidedly outclassed and was flattered by all the attention paid me. Jacques Rueff of the arresting gaze assured me that he stands straighter when he thinks of me. Professor Vallery-Radot says he's written a book explaining that at the end of your life you should abandon your profession and turn to something else. Which is exactly what I've done.

And yet I go through moments of panic when I don't know what will become of me. What if I'm making a fool of myself? I have to be more sympathetic, more patient with small talk about things that don't interest me. I've got to play according to the rules of my new profession: be amusing, be with it. I retreat into my shell too quickly when I don't feel any communication with people. Before I didn't give a damn. I knew I'd be up there on stage the next day making love to my audience. That's what I lived for. But not anymore. If I'm not affable and I don't respond, they're going to give me the cold shoulder, call me a sad old ham. I've come to the conclusion that I've got to start prodding myself, and it's not going to be easy. I've always cut a pretty poor figure in society.

But who said you had to be the life of the party, imbécile? *Don't bother trying; you'd make a spectacle of yourself. Just try being a little friendlier, that's all. When you were still singing, people didn't expect too much of you on the cocktail circuit. But you've stopped singing now, and the least you can do is talk!*

As you can see, this fallow period has had its ups and downs for me. But whenever I hit bottom, something comes along—an article or encouragement from a famous person—to save me from disaster.

Over lunch yesterday in Louveciennes, at the house of the publishing magnate Pierre Lazareff, Monsieur Georges Pompidou said to me with a smile, "You're the man we should make ambassador to Washington!"

I was really floating after that.

Professor Vallery-Radot sent me a copy of his book, *Memoirs of a Nonconformist.* It could almost have been written for me personally. At this point I'm still worried about the awful gulf that leaving the stage has opened up before me, and I have to keep reminding myself that life —or, rather, death—has left me too little time for self-pity. As long as I don't disgrace myself in the eyes of others I have nothing more to lose. The day may come when the movies and television no longer want me, when I'll have nothing but my writing to console me. I'll still come out ahead. I can still bow out proudly, knowing I've parted this life in style, before anything dreadful happened.

As long as fate leaves me a modicum of sight and sanity, I'll keep on going. Even if I'm confined to my bed, I can take courage from the example of Colette and Matisse and others who ignored their infirmities and went on growing till the end.

Such thoughts are far from cheerful, but at my age you have the right to dread those famous "bills." When you've spent a life creating and forging ahead in a profession, you don't like sitting still. You're afraid you'll stiffen up. You want to be useful.

I had tea a few days ago with Charles Percy and his wife on their way through Paris. He's a young man I much admire and in whom I place great hopes. Your role, he said, is to give us your warmth as a Frenchman who over the years and through all the storms has never lost the world's affections—even in France, and that's saying plenty!

Another evening at Paul-Louis Weiller's, this time with Monsieur and Madame Georges Pompidou, Warren Beatty, Elsa Martinelli, Artur Rubinstein, plus, once again, Salvador Dali.

Ah, and Brigitte Bardot. I didn't know she'd been invited. She walked in, taller than I remembered her, and made a beeline for Monsieur Pompidou. He kissed her hand and they began to talk, both of them smiling and very relaxed—especially Brigitte. She was wearing a wig and looked like the lovely young woman she is. Her recent photographs with her hair long and uncombed made me think she was returning to the old look.

I was standing not far from Monsieur Pompidou. When Brigitte glanced at me, I held out my hand and smiled. The response was friendly but no more. I wasn't sure if she had recognized me, because she turned back to Monsieur Pompidou without addressing another word or look in my direction.

I moved on and joined other groups. A friendly conversation with Warren Beatty, Elsa Martinelli and especially Madame Pompidou, seated at my left at table, soothed my aching complexes.

Had Brigitte given me the cold shoulder? Had she snubbed me or not?

I didn't stay to find out. Suddenly I felt out of place in this high society and crept out after coffee.

Now I know I wasn't meant to be a social animal, except in certain circumstances. I love to receive the people I like under my roof, and the success of these occasions has been heart-warming.

But at big first-nighters the cold sea of faces physically turns me off. I was made for entertaining these people, not for socializing with them. I've run into too much indifference, real or sham, and I can't get used to it.

Say there, just between the two of us, are you sure you're not still suffering from your run-in with Brigitte? If you start getting sensitive, Momo old boy, you can count on a lean old age.

Every year the P.E.N. Club organizes a special sale at which famous writers autograph their books for the general public. The sport is to see who earns the most for charity. I agreed to take part this year as a favor to my editor and as a way of thanking him for his support. My two salesladies were Suzy Volterra and Frédérique Hébrard, both familiar to the public, the first because of the brilliant comeback of her husband's stables and the other because she's a talented writer as well as Louis Velle's wife and the daughter of André Chamson of the Académie Française.

Among the other participants were greats like Edgar Faure, Gaston Monnerville and Jacques Rueff, about fifty of us all told. The sale went on from three to seven, four long hours of signing away and appealing to people's generosity.

We were ahead from the start. During the battle of the ballpoint I urged my salesladies on like a jockey driving his winning horse. The result? We came out first, not by a nose but by twenty lengths, and proudly placed in the coffers of charity more than a million old francs—or ten thousand new francs, if you must, but the other sounds much better!

This morning in *Le Figaro* there was an article about the sale. "Two Winners at the P.E.N. Club Sale," the headlines announced: "Politics and M.C."

That's pretty encouraging for a fledgling writer! (*So what are you beefing about?*)

Henri-Georges Clouzot's film *La Prisonnière* is a great box-office success. Real sadistic perversity carried to its height—that's the black genius of Clouzot. And not as immoral as you'd think, because the movie ends tragically, with a suicide. Minor maniacs may be restrained on this account, but I doubt that it will affect the major ones. Nothing can save them.

Things are really changing in the world of films. Old Clouzot will make a mint off this one. And yet in real life he's a charming man and so kind to the people he likes.

I guess I'm just lovesick. I've called off the romance between me and my public. Me, who lived and suffered and struggled for the one beautiful moment when I was up there on stage and could feel the electricity running between us—that marvelous "certain feeling."

Everything will be all right. I *know* I've made the right decision. I *know* it's always better to leave five minutes early than to outstay your welcome. But before I've completely convinced myself of this fact as far as my career is concerned, there will be a few more times when my past rises up to haunt me and to make me miserable.

A year ago an award was established in Sweden called the "Swedish Springtime Award." The trophy, a statuette of two chaste nude figures, is meant to encourage the best of the year's new crop of actors by singling out their work. For this year 1968 the three laureates were Francis Weber, a very young actor; the lovely new star Olga Georges-Picot; and the third, chosen unanimously—Old Momo, for youth and originality throughout his long and unique career.

Receiving my Swedish Springtime Award at the official ceremony next to those two babes-in-arms brought to mind my own twenties, way back when . . .

On the annual *Nuit du Cinéma,* I found myself being cited for "A triumphant international career." Mireille Mathieu, adorable in a long and shimmering dress, handed me the award while the two masters of ceremonies, Claude Dauphin and Pierre Louis, looked on. At the end of the presentation speech Claude Dauphin, that great actor and master of cool irony, had tears in his eyes. I patted his cheeks like a brother and kissed him. Then I did the same to Pierre Louis and, naturally, Mireille. In my acceptance speech I stressed the firmness of my decision to leave the stage and repeated my ambition to do some shows for international television. And I ended by revealing a secret desire to make a movie with Mireille Mathieu, in which she'd play my sister, or perhaps my daughter or granddaughter, or—most sensational of all—my mother!

I've insisted so hard on my decision that I can't go back on it now without being severely criticized. Besides, it has accomplished what I wanted: it has simplified my life.

Maurice Escande, in charge of the administration of the Comédie Française, suggested that I do two or three galas there at the beginning of March, 1969. This was the first time that a music-hall performer would be so honored in the House of Molière, and I accepted enthusiastically. But then I began to be plagued by doubts. What if people thought this meant that my farewells had been a bluff? I have my hecklers, like everyone else.

So with heavy heart I called the whole thing off. "I can't say that I think you're right," Maurice Escande replied, and then added affectionately, "But if you really feel that way, we won't talk about it any more—for the time being."

I have good days and bad, recovering from my love-sickness, but my resolve remains firm. I seem to be suffering through a moral crisis, a period of melancholy. Requests to make speeches pour in from all quarters. I refuse each one politely. It's got to be all or nothing.

Paid a call on Father Boulogne, the first successful French heart-transplant case. We had been chatting for half an hour when Professor Dubost, the surgeon who had performed the operation, burst in and said, almost shouting, "Look who's here!"

It was unbelievable. Slowly and clearly Father Boulogne described to me his terrible suffering before the sensational operation: a first heart attack, then tuberculosis and four years in a sanitarium, then several more heart attacks bringing him this time to death's door, and finally the miraculous transplant.

Professor Dubost is handsome, healthy, full of energy and as simple and outgoing as a football coach. He and Father Boulogne talk to each other in slang. During one of their discussions, about someone they don't like, Father Boulogne said to his doctor, "Don't worry, Professor, the guy's a real loser." I sat in the middle feeling a bit suffocated by the energy of this frocked ex-cadaver and his irreverent savior. They seemed like two vestiges of the good old days completely readjusted to our times, times that leave me amazed, appalled, bewildered.

There he sits, Father Boulogne, with a new heart inside him, his day already organized around the flow of visitors, nurses and mail. He gets letters from all over the world. Not to mention a succession of photographers and television cameramen whom he admits without a murmur, because he wants to do all he can to popularize the idea of heart transplants. What a great man! Throughout his busy resurrection he maintains a degree of calm that makes you wonder whether they didn't give him new nerves while they were at it.

At the end of the visit we kissed each other, me of course full of germs, he full of all kinds of medicine; and when I came to myself again I was standing outside the hospital wondering if I hadn't dreamed the whole thing.

So our heart is nothing but a pump, and our organs pipes and overflow basins. Everything making up our personalities—talent, courage, cheerfulness, pride and all the rest—comes from the brain, and everything below the neck is plumbing.

And all these years we've been singing hymns to the heart. Heartache, so dear to my heart, heartsick, my heart's an open book, heartbreak. How we've deluded ourselves!

The day they start transplanting brains, that's when we'll really have problems.

I always see things in terms of black and white. One minute I believe in my projects, next minute I'm doubtful. That's when I panic and start preparing for the worst.

And what if it happens? I'll just have to simplify

everything—my life, my ambitions, my relations with people—and make a quiet exit, humble but proud of my accomplishments.

Before I go, though, I would like to write a good book on my search for inner peace and present it as the last bow of a circus performer retiring to the wings.

People are always asking me to make guest appearances. Most of the time I manage to excuse myself, but still I find myself caught in a little whirlwind of activity. Marcel Bleustein-Blanchet, head of the biggest advertising agency in France, has set up a fund called the Vocation to help talented youngsters starting out in their professions. Recently I attended the prize-giving ceremony to present a budding architect with his award and to say a few words of encouragement to the young. I was preceded by Jacques de Lacretelle, who delivered a eulogy on the great writer and stylist André Maurois, and by Maître Floriot, who presented the various candidates with his usual grace. Following these two was no easy task, but I managed to acquit myself not too dishonorably. In my short speech I remarked that although the young during the so-called *Belle Époque* may have lived at a more relaxed time, they did not have the advantage of generous institutions like the Vocation.

Robert Manuel and his pretty young wife Claudine Coster invited me to dinner in their lovely house in

Neuilly. I haven't gotten over it yet. Manuel has the most fascinating house of any actor I know. He's obsessed by Molière and has hundreds of busts and statuettes representing our most famous comic playwright, not to mention paintings and posters of all the former greats of the Comédie Française, the whole constituting a permanent collection of theatrical memories. He even has one of my old boaters, in which he's placed a pair of Mistinguette's shoes.

The spread, from the wine and champagne to the food, was princely, a successful marriage of luxury and good taste. During the course of the dinner the two charming performers who were our host and hostess sang and recited impromptu sketches of each guest. A real show of inventiveness and imagination. I've never seen anything like it. After we'd said our goodbyes at the door I whispered to Félix and Maryse Paquet, "We had better start rehearsing tomorrow for the next party at La Louque."

Mrs. Frank Jay Gould, wife of the late American millionaire, is a great patron of the arts, especially in France. Recently she gave a literary luncheon in one of the party rooms at the Hotel Meurice. Fifty guests were invited, all of them famous: Paul Morand, Salvador Dali, Maurice Escande and on and on. On her right sat Maurice Genevoix, permanent secretary of the Académie Française, and on her left? Ma Pomme, bashful but proud of the honor bestowed on him by this *Grande Protectrice des Arts*.

Why hide the truth? I paid her sincere and shameless

court during the entire meal. In my new role and in the new world in which I'm trying to make my way, I'll need her friendship and advice. As I told her only half in jest, "In short, Mrs. Gould, you're about to become godmother to an eighty-year-old literary godchild."

She is loved and respected everywhere for the great good that she has done. She feels about France the way I feel about America. We have some things in common, don't you think, dear Mrs. Gould?

Un Mur à Jérusalem, the film by Frédéric Rossif with script by Joseph Kessel, is an impressive monument to Israeli pioneers. The rest of us can feel nothing but shame at having let the Jewish race suffer such tribulations century after century. And once again Israel is threatened with extermination! A peaceful alliance with Egypt could enrich the entire Middle East—or, at least, this was my feeling after seeing the film.

I'd like to write about an eighty-year-old who still believes in the future and be rewarded for my efforts by the encouragement he'd give to others.

Attended the twelfth annual Gala de la Piste in the Palais des Sports. This is a unique occasion for all of us who love the circus and everything equestrian. I've promised myself never to miss it.

Louis Merlin, who recently suffered a heart attack, rose from his sickbed to be master of ceremonies. He's a real trouper. Running a risk like that, he reminded me of the traveling gymnasts who perform every night without nets and every night put their lives on the line. Without people like them and Louis Merlin, the circus could not exist.

During a royal cocktail party given by Madame Derval, director of the Folies-Bergère, Marcel Pagnol looked at the actor Raymond Gérôme and whispered in my ear, "Have you ever noticed how healthy successful performers always look?"

Man of La Mancha has come to town with Jacques Brel as Don Quixote. He gives a great performance. I don't ever remember seeing a popular singer branch out the way he has. He is the rare combination of polished performer and tough and biting songwriter. The motives behind his rebellion are absolutely pure, and I'd say his future knows no limits.

Went to visit the Château de Thoiry, famous for its zoo and the lions strolling through the grounds. The day I spent there was one of the happiest of my life. The Comte de la Panouse and his son received me regally, and I promised to come back with all the children from La Louque. I wouldn't miss it for the world.

Despite all their international and domestic problems, the Americans have just proven with the triumphant mission of Apollo 8 that they are the country of the future. Fearless, heroic Captains Courageous!

For the last few days I've been suffering from a feverless flu. If I listened to my own advice I'd wait it out in bed. But I've always made it a rule to ignore my better instincts, and so I continue to make the rounds.

Had drinks with Jacques Rueff, one of the rare greats with whom I feel at ease. He's so natural you forget that he is a financier whose opinion is respected the whole world over.

There were twenty guests, all important people. I felt that they were saying to me, "We see no objection to accepting you as one of us, if you so desire." This kind of automatic acceptance is new to me. I have to keep saying to my more bashful side, *Now listen, you may be social climbing but you are also entering a new world.* I feel like a conscientious student who's been admitted into a community of kind and helpful scholars.

I dwell on this subject because of my perpetual "has-been" complex. Of course, everybody ends up a has-been to a certain extent. You can't ask for the moon. How many famous people throughout history have ended their lives in triumph? Not very many, you'll have to admit. Most of them ended up humiliated or broke, though in spite of their humble ending, they have still bequeathed to us the memory of their former greatness. So a simple craftsman like me who has peddled his wares from one end of the world to the other, who has even set some records while he was at it, and who has ended his career suddenly at the age of eighty to keep his memory bright —well, frankly, I think he is doing better than most.

Anyway, that's what I tell myself when a feeling of helplessness starts fanning my old complexes.

I forbid you to feel sorry for yourself because you can't beat yourself at your own game. I forbid you to look at yourself as if you were a last vestige of a bygone era. Until the day when somebody else accomplishes what you've accomplished, or more, you can just rest on your laurels and watch them fight it out. Good luck, kids.

You can really go nuts tormenting yourself over nothing; so let's be sensible, eh?

December 29, 1968. A phone call last night from San Francisco. It's probably my American "Daddy," Louis R. Lurie, I thought, wanting to wish me a Happy New Year. But there was more to the story than that.

First he asked me how I was. Fine, said I, but I'm impatient to get going on something. I miss the stage. I especially miss my public. Well, he said, it's never a good idea to bow out completely. You've got responsibilities. True, I said, and started talking about my television projects, due to be settled in January; and then, out of the blue, he suggested that I make a movie of my life—he'd be glad to provide the cash. I couldn't believe my ears, and I made him repeat it again. But that's what he had said: a matter of seven or eight million dollars.

Happy New Year, Daddy!

December 31, 1968. We've come to spend New Year's Eve with our friends, the Nellens, at Knokke in Belgium. The weather is terrible, ice and snow. So much for that. We shall stay five days, and the New Year begins at midnight tonight. So here's to Belgium with love!

I promised my doctor to stay off both whiskey and champagne. I'm going to suffer.

I was asked by the Belgian national radio who I would choose as Man of the Year for 1968. My answer? A big papa astronaut with three space helmets and three brave hearts.

A country can't be in such a bad way when it's first to land on the moon.

You've got to give me credit for keeping my word. I've been offered a ten-year contract in the United States for an annual farewell tour. Not even tempted. But can you imagine? What will they think of next?

January 1, 1969. Our first three days at Knokke have been accompanied by record bad weather—snow, slush and ice.

But the weather didn't discourage the crowd who came to the New Year's Eve party last night at the Réserve, a hotel owned by the Nellens. The younger generation in Belgium, I noted, was a big improvement, physically speaking, over the Belgians I used to know.

Everybody downed champagne as if it were going out of style, laughed, danced and carried on until midnight, when a drum roll and the dimming of the lights announced the coming of the New Year.

The kissing started among friends and then became pretty general. I was one of the few performers present, and before I knew it I was shaking hands and receiving three busses, an old Belgian custom. The degree of pleasure you derive from it, I discovered, is directly proportional to the age and beauty of the ladies participating.

A phone call this morning from the radio station Europe Number 1 informed me that I had been promoted to the grade of Officier of the Legion of Honor. As the first piece of news of 1969, it augurs well. My former title was Chevalier. From Chevalier to Officier, that's progress!

Cheer up, old man. Things are looking good.

When you're going on eighty-one, there is no point in trying to keep everyone in stitches. It is hard enough to keep smiling yourself.

My official religion: *Maman, Dieu* and the public. It's an all-inclusive faith, and now that I'm nearing the end I pray to keep it as pure and simple as that.

Jacques Brel came to lunch at La Louque. I was delighted by his sweetness, his self-control, and a purity that often imparts a real beauty to his Christlike face. For his role as Don Quixote he has had to let his hair grow, and the result proves that long hair can complement certain masculine features.

Is he always that calm? Or was he saving his voice for the evening's exhausting performance? He spoke very softly, a sudden gravity transforming his childlike expression when he wanted to make a point. His honesty and force of character are amazing. And think what he's going through now! He's lost several pounds since the opening of the show in Brussels and then in Paris. You'll probably smile when I tell you this, but I found Jacques Brel inspiring. He did me good. I've known so few in show business like him. He shares the desire for simplification, rather than amplification, that's come over me since I have begun charting my last course. He was like an angel of destiny, an omen.

One of the many things he said to me was that he's proud to be able to take people's minds off their worries. He likes being a pain-killer, even if only a temporary one. Like aspirin.

And why have I spent my life singing if not to cheer people up and show them the happier side of life? I got my strength from their pleasure. Dr. Sunshine. This visit with Brel reminded me of my debt to little Maurice of Ménilmontant who has stood by me all these years, even now when I really need him, and I mentally squeezed his small hand.

We will never be intimate, Brel and I; but we should meet from time to time and encourage each other simply to remain ourselves.

Here's to you, Brel.

Went to see Elvire Popesco in *La Dame de Chicago*, a kind of parody of the Al Capone era in the 1920s. The play was directed like one of Feydeau's turn-of-the-century comedies—fast, furious and funny.

The audience had a very good time. The great Elvire looked less happy. She seemed decidedly ill-at-ease in the middle of the organized confusion. Only when she was able to set the tone did she show her usual class, and even then the results weren't worth the effort they must have cost her.

Afterward I went backstage to her dressing room and found her in very low spirits, as if she were harboring some secret sadness. She seemed to be losing her foothold on life, and I felt her wonderful weary eyes looking to me for encouragement. Like everybody else she thinks I'm stronger than I am. All I could say was that she *had* to go on, that she was an inspiration to us all and that keeping up the fight was the best cure for what was ailing her.

My problems were different, I told her. When I was on stage, I was all alone except for my official accompanist, Fred Freed. No masterpiece to lean on. Just my personality and imagination and a lot of moving about. In those circumstances and at my age there was nowhere to go but down. The great melancholy Elvire nodded tenderly, as if she understood.

Her fans were waiting on the stairs for her to sign their programs. I said goodbye and got up to go. She refused to stay seated. With the help of her cane she rose to her feet and, looking at me with her indefinable gaze, bent over to kiss my hand. Instinctively I tried to stop her, to no avail. Then I kissed hers and left, tears welling in my eyes. We're two old soldiers, propping each other up with our mutual esteem and united in our love for the public.

Annual dinner at Ris-Orangis, the home that is my contribution to the old age of forgotten entertainers. It's such sweet sadness to go there and see the old, lined faces I'd known when they were in their prime! This time a new recruit added prestige to the assembly of forgotten names: Eugène Criqui, an ex-champion boxer, now seventy-five. He and his wife, both very ill, are an unexpected addition to this group of old music-hall entertainers. Why are they there? It's very simple: When he was at the height of his fame, Criqui and I staged a few mock fights for the benefit of the coffers of Ris. So I had the Criquis admitted as former benefactors of the institution. Which they are.

Criqui had asked me to find a place for them at Ris. They were willing to pay a lump sum to replace the usual installments. He had the common sense and wisdom to see that this decision would greatly simplify their old age: no more housework, cooking, taxes. They would have a comfortable room and grounds to stroll through. As far as they were concerned, this change of life would offer nothing but advantages. I agreed with them. I found him very happy with their new surroundings.

During World War I, Criqui had his jawbone smashed by a piece of shrapnel, but that didn't stop him from subsequently besting every champion who stood between him and the coveted title of world champion, so rarely earned by a Frenchman, that he won in America in his class. Now he's completely bald and as wrinkled as an old apple. His body is riddled with ailments, but the way that he still considers himself fortune's darling is a lesson to us all. I embraced him, very moved. I could still see him winning his first fights in the ring of the Élysée-Montmartre before the First World War. And his victory over Charles Ledoux, another fine champion of the times, whom he knocked out at the beginning of their fight.

I remembered these fights, right up to the world championship. Criqui was as simple then as he was at the beginning of his career, and as unassuming as he is today at the evening of his life. I can't deny that I find him most moving now. He accepts his fate as eagerly as he did when he was at the pinnacle of his glory. No bitterness. No complaining.

"We're very happy here, Maurice. No, we don't need a thing. Our luck is still with us. Everything is perfect. Come back, Maurice, and see us soon."

He's never been greater, Eugène Criqui, or more of a champion. He's the champion of self-discipline. Oh these city kids . . .

Would you be kind enough, Georges Cravenne asked me, to escort Barbra Streisand to the Opéra for the première of *Funny Girl*, a benefit performance for the charity called *Les Petits Lits Blancs*? She herself seems to like the idea a lot.

With pleasure, Georges, with pleasure. Cravenne, exultant, declared that the photograph of the two of us would make front pages the whole world over.

Well, I wasn't so sure about that, but I was very happy to have been chosen for the honor. I have known Barbra Streisand ever since she first took New York by storm, and like everybody else, I was completely bowled over. America is used to all kinds of storms, but in the almost half a century that I've had the good fortune to perform there, I've never seen anyone as young as Barbra Streisand, and so unusual, who seemed so likely to succeed.

It was arranged that I pick her up at her suite at the Plaza Athénée Hotel. Her manager and a young man from the Paris office of Columbia Pictures received me at the door. A few minutes later, she made her appearance. Or apparition. The young Jewess who looked pretty much the way nature made her when I met her on Broadway had turned herself into a Hollywood superstar. Her strange and lovely eyes glanced over at me kindly as if to say, "O.K., Maurice, what do you think of *that*?"

I told her I was delighted to see her again. She took my arm, looking highly amused, and we set off like two newlyweds in a Rolls Royce provided by Columbia for the occasion. We had to take an extra turn around the block when we got to the Opéra in order not to make our entrance too soon.

Arm in arm, we started to ascend the staircase, but there were so many photographers on all sides racing upstairs backward to get their shots, and so many young organizers hired to control them, that the whole thing became pretty comical. Finally we made it to the top; we'd been hoisted up the line of organizers almost without touching ground. I felt really sorry for the photographers.

The crowd of people pressing forward to get a better look didn't make our entrance any more majestic!

The house lights were already dimmed when we arrived, and the film had begun. The audience applauded us as spots followed our progress toward our seats. Oof. Finally we sat down. On Barbra's left was her co-star,

Omar Sharif. He speaks better French than I do, which isn't so surprising.

My part of the job was almost over and I was breathing more easily. Barbra spent the first half of the movie talking mainly to Omar Sharif, while I concentrated happily on the screen. Paris had received Barbra like the thoroughbred she is. Bravo!

Intermission. Maria Callas joined us to make a foursome for the photographers. The few words that I exchanged with the great diva made me feel singularly simple and vulnerable.

A triumph. Paris, the toughest of judges, was enchanted. The most famous people present came to shake Barbra's hand. She thanked each one politely, but I could tell she was a bundle of nerves just barely under control for the occasion. More smiles, more photographs, and then back to our seats for the second half. The battle had been won. Judaism's loveliest flower had captivated the hearts of Paris as completely as young Lindbergh did many years ago when he showed the jaded old city a sight it had never seen before.

I had excused myself from the supper that was to follow. My age, you know. I went home to La Louque highly pleased with my performance on behalf of Barbra Streisand, Franco-American friendship and international show business. *Très bien, Momo. Well done.*

Two days later we found ourselves in the north of Paris at the European Vaudeville Theater. An entirely different public, simple and undemanding. No more of the high-society types found at Opéra galas. Mothers, daughters, fathers, sons, husbands, wives and kids, storekeepers and workers from the Clichy neighborhood, they had all come to see a play called *Seuls les Tilleuls Mentent* (Only the Lindens Lie). The stars were two comics named Roger Nicolas and Pierre Doris, aided and abetted by Arlette Didier, who is as cute as a bug's ear and a real pro. The three of them served up a burlesque concoction that was absolutely irresistible. If I didn't guffaw a hundred times, my name isn't Maurice Chevalier. Anyone who sticks up his nose at this kind of show is depriving himself of some genuine Gallic humor presented with skill and verve by real masters of the art of the gag.

I found myself reliving the days when my mother, my brother and I used to go to the Folies Belleville to applaud Raoul Villot and Daudibert. Or to the Concert du Commerce in the Faubourg du Temple where Verner, Boucot and Barock had them rolling in the aisles with the same kind of belly laugh I just had the pleasure of rediscovering.

I went back to their dressing rooms after the show to congratulate the three stars for the wonderful afternoon they had given me. This was a Sunday matinee and they were going to perform again that evening. Then Nicolas and Doris were to sing in three different night clubs to round off their day of comic travail. Imagine these people and the happiness they spread among the nicest audiences in France!

You have got to be long on energy and on comic good will to distribute so much joy in this world of simple people who, like all of us, just want to forget their troubles now and then.

I check the score with myself each morning to see what progress I'm making. How complicated life seems when you try to make some sense of it!

January 22, 1969. We're at Cannes for the Midem. I've been invited to this annual gathering of people from the record and music industries to receive a special reward.

The flight to Nice from Orly airport outside Paris took only an hour and a quarter. Madame Marta Barrière, whose husband owns the casinos in Cannes, Deauville and La Baule, was waiting for us at the airport to serve as our most attractive chauffeur. The main highway from Nice to Cannes took us along the shimmering coast, and soon we found ourselves at La Croisette.

Cannes has changed a lot since I spent twenty-five consecutive summers next door in the little village of La Bocca. The city has gone modern, like everything else, but it hasn't lost its charms: sun, sea, and two arms of land wide open to receive all life has to offer. Cannes makes you glad to be alive.

On the days when I hit bottom and think I'll never do another thing worthy of my name, help arrives sometimes from unexpected sources.

I just got a letter from a federation of French engravers, a large and important group with ties in fifteen different countries. They have invited me to their annual dinner at the Eiffel Tower restaurant two months from now because they know I was an engraver's apprentice before I took up singing. But they aren't as interested in the fact that I'm a stage, screen and television star as they are in what they call my "professional integrity."

I felt a shiver of delight when I read the invitation. A group of workers and craftsmen had made me a symbol of their livelihood and devotion to their jobs. Nothing could have pleased me more.

And there's even a certain logic in the idea. After all, I have never pretended to be a great singer or—heaven help me—a genius. I have never asked to be classed with the elect. Of all the honors I've received the one I treasure most is the title awarded me by a group of prize-winning craftsmen from all the countries where French is spoken. They named me "*Meilleur artisan de la chanson française*"—"Best Artisan of French Song."

That was fifteen years ago; and now when I'm busy establishing the old balance sheet, another group of workers is helping me draw up the credit side. Thank you, engravers of France. I like the idea of representing the aristocrats of the working world. People who respect the daily grind. It goes along with the street-kid side of my nature. I wasn't born in Ménilmontant for nothing!

These people—my people—find it natural to have to struggle along. Sometimes they're good and sometimes they're bad, like everybody else, even the saints among us. I'm proud to be their spokesman. Now suddenly, at eighty, I've got my bearings again. The workers' heaven has opened its gates and voices inside are saying, "When you're ready, come as you are. Humble beginnings and all." I'm reassured.

Just spent a wonderful evening at the Midem.

During the second half of the proceedings Michel Droit announced the "supertrophy" honoring my sixty-eight years in international show business. The audience, consisting mainly of long-haired kids, received him warmly, but I could tell he was feeling out of his element. After he started to list all my titles, I realized that I had better not look too serious; the occasion called for some clowning. So when he called me "the greatest," I broke in with "Doubtful, but certainly the oldest." At another point he lost his place and I said softly, "You weren't this nervous interviewing de Gaulle" (which is what he's best known for). And so forth and so on till I'd warmed things up a bit.

The young stars being cited were all lined up behind me, and I asked permission to wish them "good luck" as a veteran performer who knew the ropes. I could tell by their expressions that it was a good idea. Then I came back to the front of the stage to say that I hoped that 1969 would be kinder to the world than 1968 had been, and the evening drew to a successful close.

Everything had been easy and satisfying, even the interviews and press conferences during the day. My stay at the Midem had gone off without a hitch and all was well with the world.

The next day the sun shone on Cannes and in my heart. I couldn't stop thinking about the engravers' invitation and what it meant to me. I felt like a new Maurice. I no longer needed my public. How could I feel heartsick and melancholy when the future held such promise? *So long, boater. When I've got the affections of everybody, young and old, humble and glorious, I don't need applause.* This is what I said to myself as I walked along, with the sun on my face, toward the brave new world where I stood for "professional integrity" among people who really knew the meaning of those two words.

What a wonderful feeling to emerge from the confusion of the past into a sunlit place where everything seems clear. My dear La Louque, you already know what I mean.

They're dying to live and dying to succeed: that's my impression of the performers who blistered my ears during two deafening evenings at the Midem. The same holds true for most young entertainers these days, not only in France but all over the world. Every time they get up on stage, it seems to be a question of do or die, succeed or perish trying, love me or I kill myself as soon as I get to the wings.

I know that Midem represents the international record industry and has to follow trends, including the revolutionary sounds and rhythms introduced many years ago by Elvis Presley and with us still.

Be that as it may, it's too bad that excellent performers have to push themselves so hard simply to survive. I wish them luck and the superhuman endurance needed to hang on. Thank goodness I never had to work so hard to earn *my* laurels!

Self-control: the hardest thing to learn. We all have instincts and urges that we have to dose, diminish, or destroy. But their workings are mysterious and they can crop right up again—a chance meeting is sometimes enough of a signal to set them off. You're upset because you can't control them and because you know how dangerous your weakness is. You find yourself in the grips of a kind of sickness that clouds your reason and leaves you momentarily bedazzled and befuddled.

What is this world coming to? Why all this universal agitation? The theater and the movies have never used such license before to teach us (that's their story) moral lessons. Babes in arms today are wise in the ways of sex and sexual deviations. People like things to be crazy, senseless. Far out.

And as fast and loud as possible.

An old man can survive simply by knowing his own limitations. But what about the kids? What kind of heart and mind will this chaos put inside them? With the invention of organ transplants, they'll be lucky if they're their own. Astronautics, atoms, they've got to know everything to get by. What a job! And in their ideas of good and evil, can and can't, what revolutions there will be!

From now on, people are going to be either geniuses or nuts. There will be no more simple peasants when television has annexed the boondocks to the towns and the towns to world capitals. People are going to want to live more and more dangerously, and I feel sorry for them already. Once upon a time they were glad just to be alive.

This in-between period in my life has begun to get me down more than I'd like to admit. Nonetheless I'm beginning to see clear in the maze of thoughts clouding my old brain.

I'm over eighty in a world where the young reject the old with more intensity than ever before. So what should an old man do? Fight to stay in the limelight? Try to impress the world when he doesn't even understand what it wants any more?

Don't. Don't put a blot on your record. It's too late to be harboring any illusions. Face the facts: At your age you don't go chasing rainbows. And the world musn't see you begging for special favors. Just take a look around you and compare your old age with other people's. You're scandalously lucky.

Clean out the cobwebs with all the strength of mind you've got left. Keep your sights clear. The most important thing is never to be ashamed; you can't ask for more.

And the most wonderful thing is to have the wisdom to recognize what you can no longer hope for, what you no longer merit. Understand, accept the facts and then go on from there. No regrets now, and no wailing and moaning. Remember Kismet, *Momo my boy, and learn to give up gracefully.*

The former Théâtre Sarah Bernhardt has been completely remodeled into a noteworthy municipal theater called, logically enough, Théâtre de la Ville (City Theater). Of the several shows given there daily, I especially wanted to see the one in the six-thirty to seven-thirty slot: Guy Bedos and his wife Sophie Daumier, two of the most attractive, funny and perceptive people in the music-hall world. As for the theater itself, well, I found it a bit too much like an arena for my tastes. Inspired by similar experiments in the United States, it's a bit too high and too wide. I felt lost in the crowd. Contact was difficult, and I didn't get my usual pleasure from the performance of this young couple; I think there was just too much space between us. But before I write the theater off, I should really take in an evening show. It's a wonderful idea to have constructed this municipal theater, and we have every reason to want it to succeed.

In the old days I used to go watch Eugène Criqui fight in the ring at the Élysée-Montmartre. If anyone had told me then that one night decades later I'd return to see a play performed there, I would have laughed right in his face. But it's true. Jean-Louis Barrault has staged his play *Rabelais* at the Élysée-Montmartre. The press reviews were excellent; so one Saturday recently I went to see the matinee performance of this kind of "Impossible Dream."

Probably everybody knows that Jean-Louis Barrault was the director, with his wife Madeleine Renaud, of the state-subsidized Théâtre de France at the Odéon until June 1968. That's when he got into trouble. Because he had been a little forward during the events of May and June, the government showed him the door during its time of reckoning with the "activists" after the crisis passed. Out of a job, he had to think of something to sustain himself as well as an act of bravura. And the result is *Rabelais,* conceived, written, directed and produced by him in a place that seems totally unsuited to the dramatic arts!

I wasn't taking sides in the Barraults' tiff with the government; I just wanted to show my sincere and affectionate admiration for them. And I was curious to see their effort to keep their place in the theatrical firmament of Paris despite their recent humiliation.

A stroll from the Place Clichy to the Square d'Anvers, where the theater is, gave me a chance to breathe in the atmosphere of Montmartre that changes with every European upheaval. When I got to the Élysée-Montmartre I found there were separate posters and box offices for the two offerings of the house: wrestling matches and *Rabelais.* And lines had formed for both. It was hard to take the whole thing seriously.

We picked up our tickets, climbed the stairs, and went into the house. I felt as if I hadn't been there in a hundred years. Already there were a surprising number of people for a Saturday matinee on a sunny afternoon. In the middle of the audience was a kind of platform in the form of a "T" covered with a worn carpet. There were no projectors or sets in evidence. My throat tightened. How unappealing. It looked like a flea-bag operation.

The house-of-all-trades was filled to cracking when Jean-Louis Barrault came over to thank us for being there. Only natural, I said. The lights dimmed. Spotlights picked out books scattered all over a corner of the stage and a group of men standing around them and talking loudly, as if in a public forum. The lines, spoken rapidly and well, held you from the start. Suddenly a man appeared in a blaze of light at the far end of the platform. The action took over and never let up for a second. The play of lights made you forget there were no sets: the stage was filled with Rabelais, a certain rhythm and tone, and talent by the trainload. A troupe of pretty girls, who acted as well as they danced, livened up the proceedings. The finale of the first act was a triumph of modern theatrical technique: the lovely, graceful movements of the girls and the blinking of the projectors provided all the punch necessary to guarantee success. The audience clapped wildly.

Some American students and a few others asked for my autograph. The widow of the playwright Paul Claudel was there with one of her daughters; I went over to greet them.

The second act began, and the miracle continued through the end. The comedian Virlogeux, who played Panurge, was brilliant, and so was Dora Doll, an ex-singer turned actress who is profiting from her well-preserved attractions and the talent she's developed over the years. The whole thing was a triumph. Barrault passed on and off the stage, his features transfigured, now with the troupe, now alone. At the end he was a lone figure facing the public he had knocked out with the same finesse shown by generations of champions on the very same platform!

I rose to my feet to applaud the magnificent creative performance of this man who has earned the respect and admiration even of people who disagreed with his stance during the famous events of May, 1968. He hasn't campaigned; he hasn't asked for pity. He has fought back with the weapons most natural to a great actor and director, and has proved while he was at it that he is a master among masters. The public is rewarding him for his courage. Bravo Jean-Louis Barrault!

Three Men on a Horse has opened in Paris and ought to be with us for a long long time. Simone Berriau, director of the Théâtre Antoine, is the lucky hostess to this good old-fashioned hit. It would have drawn crowds fifty years ago, it is drawing them today, and I have no doubt it will be doing as well fifty years from now. An American hit of the 1930s brilliantly translated and adapted—and wonderfully acted by some genuine comics, Robert Dhéry in the lead—it gives you a laugh a minute. Well done, boys and girls.

Frank Borman, one of the three American astronauts almost to touch the moon, is making a good-will tour of

Europe. Radio Luxembourg asked me to be at the Hotel Crillon to greet him when he got to Paris.

Everything was ready. The hero of the hour had arrived. America had sent us its handsomest son. I straightened; he came toward me with his hand outstretched. When I started to speak, he took the words right out of my mouth with an enthusiastic "Sir, it is a great honor to be able to shake your hand." He told me he was one of my fans. I practically fainted with pleasure but managed to pull myself together enough to blurt out in my best English all that was in my heart. So now we were buddies. I told him that he'd be seeing me again in an hour because His Excellency Sargent Shriver had asked me to come to the reception for him at the American embassy, and I added that I hoped he didn't get the feeling that I was dogging his every footstep!

At the embassy there seemed to be a thousand people ahead of me in line to shake our hero's hand. I could see him at the other end standing next to his pretty wife accepting their congratulations as modestly as a worker getting praise from his boss. Finally it was my turn. Mrs. Shriver kissed me on both cheeks. I told her husband that Borman and I were already pals, and then there I was in front of the lovable kid and his wife. I could tell by their faces that they knew how much M.C. loves America. I felt like a charged battery. Those two beautiful open faces, those affectionate looks! "Uh oh," I thought to myself, "there goes another night of sleep."

On the front page of this morning's *Le Figaro* there's a big photograph of the Ambassador, Mrs. Shriver, Papa Maurice—and Frank Borman and his wife looking at me tenderly.

Tell me, Lord. What have I ever done for you to deserve such special treatment?

I'll make a handsome exit if I can just go on acting the way I am now for as long (or as short) as I live.

I'd like my old age to be my best performance, and I'm going to start working on it right away by cleaning the skeletons out of my closet. Now's the time to do it, before anything else stupid or ugly or disagreeable can get a toehold on me. I've done with my skeletons; they've bothered me once too often. That's the way I feel at this moment of reckoning when I've decided how to arrive at peace and serenity, my last goals. And my last reward.

I'm going to try to recapture the simplicity of my Ménilmontant beginnings and then just glide along toward my final bow.

I know I'm repeating myself, but I want to say it again: All my life my public has been the thing I cared most about, after my mother. It's rewarded me and consoled me ever since my beginnings. Now that I find myself on the verge of saying goodbye to it forever, it's pretty natural to want to leave it with happy memories of me.

Why should I want to run when the time has come to walk slowly and watch very carefully where I put my feet?

When you're part of the entertainment world, you run into a lot of journalists, masculine and feminine, during the course of your career. And sometimes—hopefully not too often—you have the disagreeable experience of talking frankly to one of them and then reading an article which completely twists what you've said. When that happens, you kick yourself for having been so obliging and promise yourself never to fall into that trap again.

But recently I've been particularly fortunate in that department. Thanks to three women journalists I've had to revise my opinion of the whole profession.

The first to interview me was Vera Faure from a Versailles newspaper. She's a young and wholesome brunette beauty, a pleasure to look at, and our conversation went well from the very start. The photographer who came with her was quick, adroit and discreet; her interesting questions made answering easy. I find that these things always turn out better if the subjects brought up in the interview are appropriate and intelligently chosen.

In short, I felt in my element, and our hour together seemed like minutes. The article that came out of it was a faithful account of our conversation. Maybe I've made a new friend of that newspaperwoman. From now on I put myself at her disposal.

Then came Jacqueline Chabridon, who works for Philippe Bouvard, a highly successful young journalist of our times. She is an astonishing young woman. She has the face of a wide-eyed kid, the figure of a model and an intelligence really surprising for someone her age. Her experience derives from the fact that she has to meet all sorts of people, usual and unusual, in her daily search for news.

While I was in Cannes for the Midem she and I spent hours together chatting about this and that and the result was a terrific article on Bouvard's page of *Le Figaro.* I was so pleased I did something I've made it a rule not to do: I telegraphed my thanks.

Any time, dear Jacqueline Chabridon.

My third happy surprise came yesterday: France Roche from the newspaper *France-Soir.* Our appointment had been set by telephone and I was not looking forward to it. We had met before and for one reason or another had not hit it off. Our relations were polite but not much more than that.

But this time something clicked.

France Roche is a pretty and elegant woman, and when she walked into my living room I almost told her that nobody had the right to be that attractive and a good newspaperwoman too. I was impressed and a little intimidated. But I was wrong to be afraid. We talked for two hours straight without once looking at our watches, and night was falling around La Louque when we decided that we had better stop.

The article hasn't appeared yet, but I'll be very sorry if it doesn't reflect the atmosphere of humanism and mutual understanding that I felt during our interview.

So there you are, ladies and gentlemen. That's what three lovely lady journalists of today can do for an old party who suffers from horrible inferiority complexes every time he has to talk to someone he suspects of being "intellectual." Or maybe—do you suppose I'm making progress?

What a contrast with some of the interviews of the past

with journalists who harbored an expression of unutterable boredom while they took down answers to questions that must have embarrassed them as much as they did me. After surviving an hour that seemed like a century, I then had to endure the added indignity of the article that came out of it, in which I was presented as a Nothing by the great Mr. Journalist who had paid me the honor of annoying me for an hour and then earned his bread by cutting me down to size.

So thank you, ladies, for transforming this ordeal into a pleasure.

I think—I hope—that I'm navigating this period in my life in the proper manner. I've recovered from my lovesickness. Every day I feel I'm getting closer to meeting man's most difficult challenge: the end of his life.

Montaigne talks about this problem in a long chapter called "Experience." I'm reading it right now and it has revived my common sense. He asks the following question (and proceeds to answer it with some pretty unbeatable arguments): Have you been able to think out and shape your life? If so, you have completed the most difficult task of all: "It is our duty to set certain standards for ourselves. Our greatest and most glorious accomplishment is to live in accordance with them. Everything else, be it building cities, reigning, or amassing a fortune, is nothing more than added fillips and details."

Put that in your pipe and smoke it.

A much respected man of the cloth, Father Michel Riquet, recently ended an article with one of Pascal's reflections: "The tiniest expression of brotherly love is worth more than all our bodies put together and all our souls and everything they've done. It is of an infinitely higher order."

When you've got men like these to show you the way, following the right path becomes much easier and simpler and especially more satisfying. In today's world, which has become more and more complicated and troubled despite the progress science is making, people don't need the reflections of politicians and scholars to guide them; they need the help of wise men like Montaigne who know that a man's greatest dignity lies in what he makes of himself. Regardless of his wealth or station.

Why so serious, you're thinking? I ask you: Isn't it about time I started getting serious?

Another dramatic situation in the entertainment world: the trials and tribulations of Barrault–Renaud. Madeleine Renaud is currently playing in the Théâtre Gémier in the Palais de Chaillot, where I went to see her and Claude Dauphin give magnificent performances in Marguerite Duras' *L'Amante anglaise* (The English Mistress). The two of them are absolutely alone underneath the spotlights that serve to intensify the questioning nature of the play.

Afterward I went backstage to Madeleine Renaud's dressing room. Her husband was waiting for her. I could tell from talking with them that they were both suffering despite their present successes. He is afraid it will be impossible for him to take *Rabelais* on tour because of the expense of moving a big company around; and she has had to go off on her own because there was no part that fit her in her husband's extraordinary play. The results—for which we can be grateful—are her performances in the movie *Le Diable par la queue* (Catch a Devil by the Tail) and here, on the stage.

Two of our greatest theatrical stars have been forced to change all their plans because of political decisions on both sides that nobody can be proud of. The enthusiasm that has greeted their recent efforts hasn't made the bitter pill any easier to swallow. Thank goodness for the independence of the music-hall singer, particularly when his specialty is one-man shows!

At one of our recent midday gatherings at La Louque, Louis Armand of the Académie Française presented me with the insignia of an Officer of the Legion of Honor. "By virtue of the powers with which I've been entrusted . . ." He accompanied the presentation by a little speech on the subject of the smile, the phenomenon which separates men from beasts. He started by mentioning the first smile that a baby makes at its mother and ended by describing the smile with which I had infected the world.

So now I can officially wear my red rosette, and my lapel can blush with pride *toujours*.

I still chafe at doing nothing, but I'd be more unhappy if I didn't keep hearing how impressed people were by my leaving the stage. Besides, what with the wide screen and television, radio and books, there are still plenty of ways for me to communicate with my public. Self-pity will only get me down.

So stop complaining, Momo.

Félix Paquet and I took a stroll recently through Saint-Germain-des-Prés to check up on the progress of the younger generation.

To tell the truth, you see fewer dirty, bearded eccentrics than reasonable-looking students properly dressed. Their hair is still longer than I am used to, but it's shorter than before. Lots of them recognized me and came over with their hands outstretched or smiled in a friendly fashion. A young black woman with a lovely face came up to me to ask me for my autograph. The ravishing creature thanked me with an affectionate smile.

Then we came up to a flower vendor who stopped dead in the middle of arranging a bouquet of flowers and burst out, "*Mais . . . c'est Maurice Chevalier.*"

I answered, "*Mais oui. Bonjour, madame.*"

And she responded, blushing purple, "*Oh. Bonjour, madame.*"

Véra Korène, the lovely director of the Théâtre de la Renaissance, was at the door to greet us when we came to see her current production, *Lundi, monsieur, vous serez riche* (Monday, Sir, You'll Be Rich), a musical play directed by Raymond Vogel.

The show had been well received by the critics but not by the public. Box-office sales were very slow, and Véra Korène was afraid she'd have to close the play. What was wrong with it? Too far out? No big-name stars? Some friends had sung its praises and I decided to see for myself. Well, from the very beginning I was bowled over by the Pigalle honky-tonk atmosphere of the play that took me back to the days of *Liliom* and *The Threepenny Opera* in prewar Berlin.

Action, book, music, everything blended. The story line didn't break for songs the way it does in traditional musicals. Here Antoine Duhamel's songs were sung as if they were being thought, sort of dreamily, and then merged back into the action. All the actors, or singers, or whatever you want to call them, sang the way we think and thought the way we sing. Their diction was perfection and so was their acting. In short, they've added a new technical dimension to the profession! I don't think the eight performers under Raymond Vogel's direction could possibly have done any better.

My verdict: This is an extraordinary show, as good as the other hits of the Paris season, such as *Man of La Mancha* and *Three Men on a Horse*. So why are they playing to full houses and this one not?

Because that's show business.

During intermission at one of my recent evenings at the theater an old lady seated in front of me noticed that everybody around her seemed to be glancing in my direction; so she turned her lovely, sad face toward me to have a look for herself. Finally she said, "I can't believe how much you look like Maurice Chevalier."

"*Oui, madame,*" I answered, "people say that to me all the time, but I don't mind because I like him."

She went on, "It's easy to see how they make the mistake."

The people around us began to giggle. So I added, "Of course I'm a lot younger than he is; but I don't mind if I help him to shed a few years."

The old lady smiled sympathetically. She took one last look and announced, "I never saw two people look so much alike."

Everybody laughed. The lights dimmed, the curtain went up, and despite the fact that the play was very funny, the old lady's face resumed its melancholy expression. After the play was over, I leaned across the seats in front of me and said, "*Au revoir, madame.* Excuse me for teasing you, but I so badly wanted to see you smile. The fact is—I *am* Maurice Chevalier."

The lovely old lady said that she had been glad to smile, that she didn't smile often because life had become very hard for her. And then she disappeared in the crowd slowly making its way to the exits.

We were all sorry to have made fun of her. Especially me, considering that she had overcome her great sorrow to smile in my honor.

Just saw *The Lady in Cement* with Raquel Welch, Don Blocker, and Frank Sinatra playing his old role of Tony

Rome, private detective. He does a good job despite the James Bond banality of the screenplay; he really sinks his teeth into the part of the cool, smart-aleck tough.

I have always liked both Sinatra the performer and Sinatra the man, and I think he ought to avoid playing this kind of phony hero. He's worth better than that. His singing career has been much more sensible.

It makes you wonder to see good actors who are getting along in years accept roles that they wouldn't even have looked at when they were younger. Are they forced to do it just to survive? I doubt it. I think that they simply want to seem "with it," which we all know means doing dreadful things on the stage or screen as if they were perfectly natural. And that's where I disagree with these performers. It's not necessary for them to take on roles that damage them morally. Of course, they say that an actor shouldn't be too choosy about the kind of people he'll portray because his job consists of portraying anything. Well, if this is really true, I'm glad I'm not an actor. I'd rather be the simple stage personality that I am —or was. And I'd certainly rather give up making movies altogether than end up in a state of demoralization. I probably won't be faced with the temptation, though— they aren't writing too many scripts these days calling for elderly stars to advertise the joys of immorality.

Let's try to avoid the common pitfalls of illustrious old age, Maurice. There's no point in posing as the gentleman prince, the venerable old man. Now's when you should be harking back to your origins, Momo of Ménilmontant, son of La Louque.

There may be nothing more you can add to your performance as a singer, but there's still a lot you can add to your performance as a man. And for now that means learning to accept the fact that you're almost eighty-one years old and ready to learn discretion.

In today's mail there was a letter and a book from the writer Louis Chaigne, whom I had met the other day at an exhibition. The letter is so encouraging and the book so inspirational that I feel I have a new friend to rely on. He's the kind of traveling companion that I'm looking for: someone who's going my way.

Saw, at the Théâtre du Châtelet, a lavishly updated version of *L'Auberge du cheval blanc* (The White Horse Inn). The audience was just as enthusiastic as the Châtelet crowds of yore. That created a good impression and so did the professional discipline of the company. What a contrast with the disordered world outside the theater doors! It was a rehabilitating evening.

Sol Shapiro, one of the heads of the William Morris Agency in New York, came to see me at La Louque to propose all sorts of tempting offers for the American circuit. I told him that I had said my farewells to the stage and it wouldn't look very good if I mounted it again. Sol laughed and said that Americans were used to repeat farewell performances.

"I know," I said, "and that's precisely why I don't want to start again. I don't want to be like the others."

No sir. I'm getting ready for the grand finale, the grandest one of all.

Recently we had lunch at the house of Albert Lespinasse, the manufacturer, and one of my oldest and dearest friends. There were only ten of us at table—a relatively intimate gathering. Besides the host and his wife, the group included Toty and Pilou Bardot, the parents of Brigitte; Henri Lenglet, a tall and charming businessman; Robert Manuel and his Claudine; and the Paquets and me.

Our lunch was gay despite Toty Bardot's obvious maternal concern about the escapades of her unpredictable daughter. We love and respect Toty and sympathize with her greatly—but you just can't stop Robert Manuel from cracking brilliant jokes!

On two occasions he made references to a part of my anatomy that time, alas, has bereft of its major role. He asked me to excuse him for saying so, but he thought that my autobiography had been seriously mistitled. In view, he said, of the amorous adventures it catalogues, I should have called it not *Ma Route et mes chansons* (roughly, Roads I've Traveled and Songs I've Sung) but *Ma Biroute et mes chansons, biroute* being slang for the above-mentioned member. To which he made the second reference when he suggested that my renunciation of such adventures was an event of such tragic significance that the name of the charming little village where I live should be changed from Marnes-la-Coquette to Morne-la-Quequette, which is more or less equivalent to "droopy peg."

Well, I wish you would explain the general merriment to me, because there are some jokes I'm still to young to understand.

I want to behave sensibly, and I try to be discreet, but I find that I am not always doing very well. There are too many temptations and too much confusion in the world around me. My only comfort is knowing I'm not alone. It seems as if everybody alive on this planet has thrown all the old ideas of good and bad to the winds and is proceeding rudderless through a furious storm.

Gisèle d'Assailly is dead of a stroke. When I heard the news all I could say was "oh," but I could feel that "oh" reverberating through my entire body. She and her husband René Julliard had been my friends and literary patrons, and I'll be lost and lonely without them.

One by one the people that I loved and needed are disappearing from my life. I knew them well, they knew me well. Already the younger ones have a vaguer idea than the older ones of what I was or wasn't.

But of course that's the story of everybody's life. And

everybody gets to the point where he, too, has to expect to go under. As for me, I pray the Lord to take me before I'm senile and useless. I suppose he will. Meanwhile, each time a loved one goes he takes part of me with him and leaves me more vulnerable than before. "What's the use?" I say to myself mournfully. Then slowly I recover and my spirits pick up.

It's amazing. Life gives us plenty of reasons to be miserable, and still we go on absorbing the blows until the day we're knocked out for good. Then it's our turn to demoralize the people who loved us and needed us.

We went to the Mass held for Gisèle d'Assailly at the Église Saint-Thomas d'Aquin. When I came up to her coffin I felt myself staring at it as if staring could bring her back to life.

Then I remembered the words a priest had said to me the other day when we lunched alone: "Ready yourself by accomplishing everything you can." Well, Gisèle had done all she could. And I should spend the rest of my life trying to do the same. That would be my way of trying to satisfy myself and of honoring all the people who have believed in me and given me moral support.

Adieu, Gisèle, and thank you.

I've just seen *Le Concile d'Amour* (Council of Love) on the stage and Buñuel's *The Milky Way* on the screen. People who believe in this modern delirium have lost something precious: the strength you get from faith in the power of prayer. They'll wander around aimless and flameless. Pure waste.

If anybody ever managed to sneak a television camera into the dining room during one of our La Louque lunches, he'd be rewarded for his efforts with a really good show. Yesterday, for example, the guest list included Carmen Tessier, the gossip columnist for *France-Soir,* and her husband, Ambassador Dubois; J.-J. Gautier of *Le Figaro* and his wife; Jacques Rueff and his; Georges Cravenne; the Paquets and me. As usual, I was a bit intimidated at the beginning but soon was caught up in the general atmosphere of conviviality and mutual esteem.

These luncheons are improving by leaps and bounds. I consider them a very important part of the new life I want to make for myself. So I do my best and my guests respond by doing theirs; and the result is two wonderful hours among people who get along famously and make great human music together.

Another important secret to my success: the food. If you ask people to lunch, they expect to eat; and it's up to you to see that they eat well. At my house, it's Maria, who cooks, and Maryse, who organizes everything, who get the credit for the excellent meals.

Things are pretty nice at La Louque.

It's five months now since I've sung a song. All my favorite pursuits seem to be falling victim to old age. I learned to love doing handstands and somersaults, driving a car, lots of things; and now I'm having to learn *not*

to love to do them. At the rate I'm renouncing my enthusiasms, soon I'll have none left. Ah me. I don't feel ready to be one of those old men who just sits in a corner and doesn't bother a soul.

We all knew that Jean Rigaux hadn't invited us to lunch at Lapérouse for nothing. First of all, it was his birthday and his wedding anniversary combined. Second of all, Roger Topolinski, owner of the restaurant, was looking for a way to publicize the hundredth anniversary of his famous establishment. So, tit for tat, he provided Rigaux with the lunch, and Rigaux, a famous Montmartre comic singer, provided the celebrities—that is, us, the people who assembled for apéritifs and lunch: Marcel Pagnol, the singer Tino Rossi, the writer Guy de Cars, the manufacturer Albert Lespinasse, the journalist René Lignac, their wives . . . and me. We are all the kind of friends who buss when we meet, and you should have seen the bussing!

What followed—apéritifs, food, wine, champagne, liqueurs—got everybody going, and before we knew it we were going loud and fast. Don't ever try to argue with Jean Rigaux; he could outshout the marching band of the Garde Républicaine. He has a lot to teach those student orators about making themselves heard. That day he could have drowned out a whole sit-in of them, after all the wine he'd drunk.

Marcel Pagnol doesn't get louder by the glass; he gets softer and more sentimental. Finally his lovely little wife Jacqueline decreed that things had gone far enough, that if he and I had known each other so well and for so long, it was about time we said "*tu*" to each other instead of the formal "*vous.*" So we started right in, a bit hesitantly at first, and then with great enthusiasm.

It was a Rabelaisian luncheon. After four zany hours we rose to our feet, our gaits wobbly but our hearts and stomachs replete.

It's a rare lunch these days that lasts that long; most start at one and end at two-thirty or three because everybody's in a hurry. But at Jean Rigaux's lunch at Lapérouse, we all, er, lost track of the time. That's what kind of party it was.

All my life I've had the habit of checking up on myself each morning to assess what I've said and done and been for the past twenty-four hours. This kind of tally sheet is much harder to keep when you're eighty. You lose your grip on things. You're no longer a player in life's important games; after a certain age your participation is no longer considered an asset. You learn to sit on the sidelines graciously accepting tokens of respect from the crowd. And thanking your lucky stars you still have the energy to cheer the home team on!

Eisenhower is dead, still called Ike in spite of all his official titles.

As a general he outshone all our marshals. As President

of the United States he governed for eight years and was loved and respected by his countrymen and people all over the globe. He was a fine leader in every respect.

He recovered from heart attacks as if they were colds. He had colectomies and fought his way back to health. Ike Eisenhower was a miracle of courage, but he got to the point where his courage couldn't help him. At seventy-eight he fought his final battle against an army of diseases determined to defeat him: his seventh or eighth heart attack, intestinal occlusion, pneumonia. His heart slowed down, stopped fighting, and that was that. The battle is over; he's gone.

I had met him several times. Once I breakfasted with him and the French Ambassador Hervé Alphand in the Oval Room at the White House. Another time he and Mamie and several friends asked me to join them for dinner. I have several souvenir photographs of the occasion that make my heart leap every time I look at them. Ike was a model and an inspiration to me, my ideal man. He wasted away toward the end but even then his state of exhaustion didn't prevent him from smiling death in the face as if he wanted it, too, as an ally.

I just sent his wife a cable: DEAR MAMIE, HE WAS CHEERFUL AND SMILING TO THE END. HE WAS AND WILL ALWAYS BE MY AMERICAN WONDER OF A GENTLE GIANT OF A MAN. MY WARMEST THOUGHTS ARE WITH YOU GREAT AMERICAN MAMIE LADY. MAURICE CHEVALIER.

Il y a encore des noisetiers (There Are Still Some Hazelnut Trees), the latest by Georges Simenon, is an enchanting book. I've sent it off to my Hollywood agent, who speaks French, in the hopes that he'll pass it along to the director William Wyler, who also speaks French. You see, I find there's a terrific role there, with minor adjustments, for a certain octogenarian I know; and I don't see that there's any harm in branching out a bit and doing something different. Nothing extravagant of course, just anything that might be going for a willing old man.

Tchao, the new offering by Marc Sauvajon at the Théâtre Saint Georges, has started off with a bang. It's a funny play, but the real magic of the evening lies in the dramatic chemistry of Pierre Brasseur and Elisabeth Wiener. He is monumental, she is already a ravishing bundle of talents—they're the reigning couple of the day.

Saw the controversial pop singer Antoine performing in a dinner jacket, and nobody can wear it better. He's on the right road to a brilliant future. He's not ready yet for the International Big Time; his delivery lacks polish and muscle. But with his natural charm, good humor and engaging appearance, he may be the star of the Seventies. He's got all the ingredients for a Prince Charming of pop song—provided he gets rid of the long hair and mustache!

Also he shouldn't limit himself to songs of his own composition. That's a big mistake. Singers should perform only their very best stuff and then rely on professional songwriters for the rest of the material that fits in with their style. The public couldn't care less that you write all your own songs. A good song is a good song; a good performance is a good performance. And what a popular singer needs most is really popular songs.

There may still be some French showgoers who remember Georges Roger. He was a friend of my youth and a big strapping boy. We shared a taste for American music and tap dancing around the turn of the century. Our lives were soon to take different paths, but our friendship never faltered. Georges led an adventurous existence despite an early bout of hemoptysis that we all thought would be the end of him.

The fates were kind to Georges. He came back from a long rest in the south of France as fit as ever and able to resume a career of dancing and traveling that lasted fifty years without a single recurrence of his illness. He sent me his news from time to time, but recently I realized that it was several years since I'd seen him and decided to go pay him a visit.

He lives in Deuil-la-Barre, to the north of Paris. The first time I made the trip, several weeks ago, nobody answered the doorbell. But then nobody expected me, because I had hoped to surprise him. I suppose he was sitting alone in his little house and couldn't hear my ring. In any event, I went away depressed by the ominous silence that had greeted me.

I have just come back from my second visit. This time a telegram preceded me. So I was met at the door by

Mercedes, Georges' friend who has devoted herself for the last three years to making his old age comfortable. Georges was inside where it was warm. As I entered, he stood up to greet me, leaning on his cane and looking at me with those beautiful eyes made to seem even bigger by thick lenses. We kissed each other and sat down at his modest table. Félix, whom he knew and liked from the old days, was with me. We all felt we were among friends.

Georges and I started our conversation on the subject of our gay youth and the time we spent haunting the Boulevard de Strasbourg and the Faubourg Saint-Martin, two important arteries of the Paris entertainment world. Then we got around to more relevant matters, like our present state of affairs. Georges told me that he had lived alone for ten years in this house, in ill health and totally uncared for. Finally he had managed to convince his old friend Mercedes to share his lonely existence, and he can't believe his luck. His only remaining physical activity is a twenty-minute walk, morning and evening, from one room to another to exercise his failing legs. When the weather is nice he goes out, but now it's too cold and he's very fragile.

I looked. I listened. And I found him just as wonderful as ever. Only one difference: my great big brawny friend of yore has become a wizened old man of eighty-eight eating the last crumbs of life with infinite delectation.

I told him about my stepping down from the stage, a decision he totally approved of. We discussed my dreams and projects, the recent confusion in my thoughts, and my growing conviction that at my age I should be going into reverse—back to my beginnings—rather than charging forward into the unknown.

Looking at each other tenderly, we talked and talked for two hours straight. Finally it was time to go. I promised to come back when the weather improved. And the minute I got back to La Louque I sent him a big photograph and albums of my French and American records.

I was very impressed by his realistic and smiling acceptance of the problems of old age. I can't keep my mind off him; my old free-wheeling friend has become a kind of saint. Wonderful Georges Roger.

Robert Manuel had said these two were delighted at the idea of lunching at La Louque; so that's why I insisted they come. She's Jacques Brel's partner in *Man of La Mancha;* he's the director of this near masterpiece. Both are Americans. So we decided on a Franco-American reunion at La Louque with them, Brel, the Manuels and Frédérique Hébrard as guests. At the very last minute someone telephoned to say that the composer of the musical was dying to come.

"Bring him along," I said. "We're delighted to have him." And I started to prepare for one of those La Louque luncheons that gladden my house and make me happy to be alive.

Brel, it's true, had warned me that the director was one of those people who never make compliments. He liked things or he didn't; that was his style. As for her, she was prickly too. O.K., maybe the composer would prove more amenable. And anyway, the whole responsibility was off my shoulders; it was they who had said they wanted to come. Besides, I thought I loved America enough to melt the heart of the toughest Yankee going, especially if he was sitting at my dinner table.

But from the minute they walked in I could see there would be problems.

He looked very serious and, let's say, standoffish. She wasn't exactly gushing but seemed to show more promise. I saw nothing to worry about in the composer, a big, handsome brown-haired guy, and I liked their three firm handshakes. Then we started to talk and I realized that, though they understood some French, they couldn't speak it. What was I going to do? If we spoke only French, they might feel they were missing out on things, and if we spoke only English, the Frenchmen would feel deprived. I tried a mixture of both. Conversation during the apéritif moved at a snail's pace.

A heavy silence hung over the dinner table, too. The success of my lunch was seriously threatened. Well, it was up to me to save the day because I'm the concertmaster in my house and responsible for making everybody harmonize.

I started by saying how much I was impressed with their enterprise and with the talents they displayed in it. Silence. Maybe all Americans didn't like compliments? I began to wonder. Jacques Brel (who is hardly one for flattery himself) chimed in and said that the director had greatly contributed to his own success as Don Quixote; and then he said that his American vis-à-vis was worth three French female stars. Obviously he was laying it on a bit to help me out of a bind, but his efforts did not produce the faintest sign of thawing.

Brel began to flag, and Robert Manuel took over. They

assumed the expression of three Sioux Indians who don't like the smell of a white man's deal. Félix Paquet and Frédérique Hébrard got nowhere, either.

It was my turn again. I launched into a passionate discussion of all America had meant to me since I was a boy. I told them how I loved their singers, their dancers, their boxers. I said, when an American is great, he's greater than anybody, and thought to myself, boy, you've got them there. The Americans remained unresponsive to my advances.

I had had it too. When we rose from the table the French contingent was haggard and exhausted. We all retired to the living room for coffee and suddenly I had what seemed like a brilliant idea. Why didn't we go next door and see the house Eisenhower had lived in when he was my neighbor at Marnes-la-Coquette? This would be a good ending for our reunion and a way of paying homage to a beloved American. And it might leave us with less lugubrious memories of this lunch.

But our stars were not with us. The person who had the key to the estate (now up for sale) was nowhere to be seen, and we stood shivering in the cold for half an hour while Maryse and Félix Paquet raced over to the Town Hall to find another key. Finally we gave up. We were frozen and frustrated and courting pneumonia. So we parted, in the hopes of survival.

Jacques Brel was limp with exhaustion; thank goodness he had no performance that night. Robert Manuel looked as if he had lost several pounds during the course of the afternoon. And I had some pretty harsh words with myself concerning my efficacy as French good-will ambassador.

Later on I had a reassuring thought. Every entertainer has had the experience of putting on an important performance in front of what seems like a glacial audience. He's gone home dreading the critics in the next day's papers and has woken up to a lyrical press: he's wonderful, he's never been better, et cetera.

Maybe we'll have the same delayed reaction from our American guests, I thought to myself hopefully. And sure enough, a few days later I received an enormous bouquet and an enthusiastic note.

I don't sing anymore, but I occasionally hum.

I had met the writer Roland Dorgelès at one of the cocktail parties given by our dear departed Gisèle d'Assailly, and recently he asked me to dinner at his apartment in the heart of Saint-Germain-des-Prés. I wanted so badly to go that I made an exception to my "early-to-bed" rule, a necessity now that I wake up automatically at seven and am useless all day if I haven't had a full night's rest.

But the evening that I spent with this extraordinary old man was particularly beneficial and more than made up for any loss of sleep. For one thing, there were many ladies present of a nicely ripened beauty, including his wife, who is younger than he and hovers over him like a guardian angel. And there was the Minister Louis Joxe being hearty, open and amicably official.

The conversation went along like a breeze. Louis Joxe

explains himself so naturally and clearly and talks about such interesting subjects that I soon forgot myself and plunged in with the rest. I was no longer intimidated. In fact, I began to find myself saying perfectly intelligent things.

I was unaware of time. These witty, worldly people were friendly to me. They buoyed me up. I felt equal to the situation and to them. But the real value of the evening for me was getting to know Roland Dorgelès. He's like Matisse and Colette, one of those rare octogenarians who leaves you breathless with admiration.

He admits to being eighty-two. Bad health has weakened him physically, but his spirit remains undaunted. You wouldn't believe the clarity and playfulness of his mind. His face has a kind of humorous simplicity, and he announces the coming of each joke by the twinkle in his eye.

Imagine the courage of this old man. His lamp is dimming but still sends out its friendly glow; his body is failing but he doesn't seem to notice. I could have fallen on my knees before him.

Four cartoons by Cabu in a recent *Journal du Dimanche* made me laugh out loud. The first one depicted Jacques Brel, his long hair framing his saintlike face, announcing that he was leaving show business. Then came the popular French vocalist known simply as Barbara, also very cleverly drawn, deciding that she should follow his example. Third was a sketch of the so-called rivals for Piaf's title, Mireille Mathieu and Georgette Lemaire, holding hands, a total of forty-five years between them. Last of all came me under my boater, blessed by Cabu with an abundance of wrinkles and made to represent the age of renouncement.

The caption read: "Whatever happens, Monsieur Chevalier, there will always be a place for you at the old-age home in Ris-Orangis." And I reply, "*Ah non alors* . . . I wouldn't dream of depriving one of those youngsters of his bed."

Little by little I've gotten used to the idea of living outside the entertainment world. I figured that if I kept on looking long enough, I would surely discover some advantages to my new life. I was right. I can get up in the morning free of the fear that I'll flop that night. I can look back with pride and pleasure at my career and remember that I started at the bottom and went all the way to the top without ever running into a serious rival. And I can say to myself that no Ménilmontant street kid ever did better.

I manage to see most of the plays that people are talking about. I'm a good audience though not too fond of disagreeable subjects. Luckily for me, cheerful plays seem to be the most successful these days. *Le Vison Voyageur*, Jean-Louis Dabadie's adaptation of the English comedy *Not Now Darling*, has provided the comedians Poiret and

Serrault with a vehicle for their ever-growing talents. Poiret started out as a classic stooge and then made his mark as a true comedian in *Cactus Flower*. I also admire Michel Serrault, though he tends to overact.

Their duel of wits kept the audience laughing from the opening curtain to the end of the play. After the performance, a lady of the shopkeeper type accosted me at the exit. I asked her what she thought of the play. "Very good," she said, "and very funny. But too tiring."

Ah, well. She was no longer in the bloom of youth.

Also saw the English play *Let Sleeping Wives Lie* by Brooke and Bannerman, adapted by Alexandre Breffort under the title *Le Coeur sous le paillasson*. The production is graced by a cast of young and semi-young performers who really whoop it up. Their energy and group spirit delighted an old veteran who likes to see the sacred flame burning in his successors. My former partner Raymond Bussières was also there adding his gracefully aging talent to the show. How nice that the whole production works so well and that the adorable Théâtre des Capucines is keeping up the traditions of its brilliant past!

Armand Massard, former champion fencer and Olympic Gold Medal winner in 1920, asked me to take part in a ceremony honoring the French champions of the Mexican Olympic games, Pierre Trentin and M.A.L. Oerter. I accepted with pleasure, though I didn't feel qualified, because I wanted to shake his hand again. I hadn't seen him since the time of his greatest glory.

I remembered him as being charming and rather tall, over six feet; I knew I'd had to raise my head to look him in the eyes. So when I got to the Aero-Club on the Rue Galilée where the ceremony was to take place, I looked all around for someone standing head and shoulders above the crowd. A man came toward me. He was about my height, five feet ten, and shook my hand in a friendly fashion. "Armand Massard?" I asked, and he answered, "Yes," his voice full of emotion.

He still stood up just as straight—but not just as tall—as ever. I began to ask myself, and finally got up the courage to ask him, where his extra inches had gone. He explained that sickness and old age (he's eighty-six) were responsible for his shrinkage. It took me a moment to recover from that.

Soon I was surrounded by the tennis champion Jean Borotra, looking rather skinny, and other former great athletes who are now sports editors for papers like *Le Figaro*, *L'Équipe* (a sports sheet) and *Le Parisien Libéré*. Most of them had won a title or two in their heyday. And then there was Georges Carpentier, still wearing the laurels of his boxing fame with style at seventy-five. We all congratulated each other on our healthy miens and talked happily about our pasts.

I was glad I had come, especially when they began to present past Olympic champions. One by one they came up to the microphone to receive the applause of the crowd. Some had kept their former fitness; some were hampered by aches and pains or added avoirdupois. And some could barely manage to hobble up to take their bows. Each one gave his name and the year and country in which he had won his Gold, Silver or Bronze medal (the holders of Bronze medals looked a mite embarrassed) and then took his place in line with the others while the audience clapped.

Georges Carpentier, who was sitting next to me, whispered to me that I too could have had my Olympic medal in boxing if I'd wanted to. He's said it before, and I always give him the same reply, that I lacked muscular strength and was too vulnerable to well-aimed blows. But of course I liked hearing him say it again; it made me feel part of this athletes' mutual appreciation society!

The ranks of genuine musical producers and directors are greatly diminished: Henri Varna just died. He could have been one of my family, I feel so sad. I'd worked with him many times over the years—at the Concert Mayol, the Empire Music Hall, the Palace, the Casino de Paris, grand old names in the Paris entertainment world.

Henri Varna had a genius for making women seem more beautiful. He was a master at harmonizing colors. He was tireless and hardy, a real Parisian stalwart.

When he reached his eightieth birthday, outside observers gave him twenty more years to live. Then suddenly he began to waste away before our very eyes. Bit by bit his strength began to leave him, but not his guts and enthusiasm; I'm sure he went down fighting. He had lived the life he wanted to live, working and earning his success.

He led a charmed life in the music-hall world. Anyone

who ever worked with him remembered him afterward as an excellent director and a faithful friend.

Adieu, cher Henri Varna.

All the performers and employees of the Casino de Paris and the Théâtre Mogador came to the lavish Mass celebrated in the beautiful church on the Avenue Marceau. All of them looked stricken. Fernandel the comedian, the singer Tino Rossi and I found ourselves seated near each other. We had each come to say goodbye to a professional we liked and admired.

Soon afterward I decided to go render him posthumous homage by seeing his last production at the Théâtre Mogador, *Vienne chante et danse.* The famous husband-wife operetta team, Marcel Merkès and Paulette Merval, were enchanting in the show. Back in their dressing room after the performance, we talked about Varna with great nostalgia.

The hour came to go home to Marnes-la-Coquette. Time will heal the wound. Little by little Henri Varna will fade from my thoughts and rejoin the group of my now defunct contemporaries who, death by death, make my own death draw nearer.

Charlie Chaplin will soon be eighty, and German television has asked me to contribute a short text for a program in his honor. This is what I wrote:

"There is no doubt in my mind that Charlie Chaplin is the greatest of all the many people who have, since the beginning of the century, devoted their lives to entertaining the public. The young vagabond that he created is moving and irresistibly funny. He's such a human character, and so appealing, that he was and still is copied and imitated all over the globe.

"Chaplin's style is immortal. I sincerely feel he complicated things unnecessarily by adding sound when the talkies took over.

"It's too bad that his glorious Charlot couldn't grow old along with us. He would have made our lives seem so much brighter."

Paris celebrated Chaplin's birthday with a revival of his film *The Circus*. We were present for the opening night and were as moved as ever by his genius. Too bad that there were not more people in the audience, because those who were there had such a good time laughing at the forty-year-old gags!

We will not see the likes of Chaplin soon again. A former member of the Fred Karno troupe in England, he had gone to Hollywood at the beginning of its heyday and owed to America his international fame as King of the Silent Screen. They say he lives in Switzerland now in the bosom of his family. I'm glad to hear it. There's no finer reward for a great performer than a proud and serene old age.

Recently we gave a luncheon at La Louque in honor of the journalist Philippe Bouvard and his young wife. Gérard Oury, the film director, came and left on the run to supervise the English dubbing of his film *Le Cerveau* (The Brain). The other guests were Michèle Morgan (who apologized for gaining the few ounces that made her seem all the more cuddly and caressable); the playwright Françoise Dorin (blooming); Jean Poiret (the most unerringly funny comedian I know); and the pop singer Antoine (who won everybody over immediately). Soon they all got the conversational ball rolling, and the Paquets and I were puffing along behind trying to catch up. It was a lunch in the modern spirit—that is to say, in the same old spirit, only speeded up. Over coffee in the living room we discussed more serious things, and a real warmth settled over the gathering. What a joy these lunches are for me! They continue my old tradition of relaxed good humor, and I consider them to be the finest creation of my waning years.

They give me what I used to get from theater audiences until six months ago. My guests have admiration and affection for me because I have the same for them. I'm glad if they leave happy with the two hours they've just spent. That's one of my rewards; the other is getting to know them better. I try to put on as sincere a performance before my new friends as the one I used to give my public.

I want them to leave liking me better than before and wanting to come back again. That was the effect my performance had in the days of my one-man shows.

During dinner Gérard Oury had several stories to tell. One concerned an episode in his acting career. After he had quit the Comédie Française he found himself drifting around the south of France with nothing to do. Someone at the Capitole, in Marseilles, where Alibert and Raimu were playing in a Marseillaise revue, asked him to come along and read a poem by Rostand in praise of the sun of southern France. He made his entrance in a fashion befitting an ex-actor at the Comédie Française and started reading the first verses in a well-modulated voice. The audience obviously didn't know what to make of him. What was all this culture doing in the middle of a popular show? They started to mumble, they booed and catcalled, and finally Oury felt a nice ripe Provençal tomato land on his head. Then another. And another. He made his exit with his head looking as if somebody had ladled *bouillabaisse* over it.

Oury ended by saying that he believed he had set a record there for tomatoes received head on. Whereupon Antoine leaped to his feet in protest. As far as he was concerned, he was the Champion Tomato Target (his beginnings as a singer had been rocky), and he didn't want anyone contesting his title.

My morale is really taking me for a ride these days. Up and down, just like a roller coaster.

One thing is certain: People are encouraging me to

write, and writing is my greatest joy at this moment in my life. That's where the ups come in.

The down periods have to do with my worries about the chronic confusion in my head. I'm afraid that I'll burn out what's left of my motor in my effort to set things straight. And yet a lot depends on my learning to think and meditate and organize my mind.

I think the crisis will pass and leave me at peace with myself. I just *seem* discombobulated; basically I know the difference between what I want and what I need.

One funny thing I've noticed: None of my friends ever asks me how I'm adjusting. Do you suppose they think I'm more resilient than I am?

Jacqueline Pagnol, wife of Marcel Pagnol, had offered me two seats at the Académie Française to see the induction of a new member. So at two sharp on the great day Félix and I were there to pick up our famous friend Marcel in his Academician's robes and march him off to the Académie. His costume, green and bedecked with medals and braid, was thirty years old, he said. He'd obviously gained weight since then! The material was so thick it looked like leather; the silky cape billowed out in the April breeze. I felt important just to be seen in his company.

We were a little early; you have to allow for Paris traffic these days. The Pagnols took advantage of the extra time to show us the two interior courtyards of the splendid Académie building where the Immortals (that's what they call the members) had just parked their cars.

New arrivals were standing around talking in groups and I realized I was looking at the owners of some of the most famous brains in France.

Jacqueline couldn't stay for the ceremony and left us in the hands of her favorite usher. He looked us over sympathetically from head to foot and deposited us in the last two seats of the second row. We felt like peasants at the Élysée Palace. The seats seemed a little bit narrow; have people gotten broader since the days of yore? Next to me sat the writer Pierre Emmanuel. He introduced himself and explained that this was a kind of dress rehearsal for him, because he was next in line to be received "under the Cupola." He'd never been inside the building before!

At three o'clock we heard a drum roll, and the Academicians appeared one after another at the head of the stairs. Then they took their places like ordinary human beings; some were even wearing business suits. Aside from the drum roll announcing each Academician, there wasn't much in the way of pomp and circumstance, and I began to feel a little bit cheated.

Why wasn't there more of a production? Nothing showy, of course, but just some simple hint of grandeur? I wasn't sure I liked this devil-may-care attitude! I noticed that a lot of them hadn't even bothered to come.

The Academicians are seated facing the public that is meanwhile staring at them. They have such expressionless faces that you feel as if you're looking at a row of painted statues. Only statues might be prettier. I began to protest to myself that there was a lack of decorum in their exaggerated solemnity.

Another problem is that the person being inducted doesn't come to the center where everybody can see him; he stays in his place, which happens to be in the back behind the Academicians, so that when he reads his acceptance speech only the audience can see him. The Academicians have their backs to him and look over our heads into space. The day I was there you couldn't even be sure they were listening, they all had such a faraway look in their eyes. Heads began to dangle—slow and heavy digestion perhaps.

Marcel Arland, who was being inducted, delivered the traditional eulogy of the person he was replacing, in this case the late André Maurois. Eulogy is maybe not the word, since he made it quite clear that he admired the man more than the writer. *Tiens, tiens.* That seemed to be waking them up. Certain Academicians began to show signs of life like pursed lips or a gleam in the eye. But nobody moved.

Arland finished and the assembly clapped politely. Another Immortal, Jean Mistler, stood up to deliver a long and witty compliment to their newest member, and the ceremony was over. Everybody got up to leave.

Apparently the atmosphere is not always this calm. Somebody told me later that Marcel Pagnol had everybody in stitches when he introduced Marcel Achard on the day of Achard's induction. I guess I'll have to come back.

I know some of the Immortals personally: Pagnol, Achard, Rueff, René Clair, Louis Armand. The last mentioned, honorary president of the S.N.C.F., the French national railroad, came over to see me that day. He said that he had just finished a lecture tour to present his new book, *Le Défi européen* (The European Challenge). He said he thought he'd set a record for press conferences, interviews and signing autographs and is really surprised that he managed to survive. A familiar story . . .

"We all know how strong you are, *cher maître,*" I said. He puffed out his chest and laughed.

It was time to retrieve "our" Marcel Pagnol and take him home. He invited us in for a drink. Finally we could unbutton and put the Cupola, the Immortals, and the Académie Française behind us. We relaxed. We guffawed at the sallies of this master playwright of popular theatrical hits. Pagnol's Provençal humor transported me back to the 1930s when I sat with the greats of the Marseilles theater—Raimu, Charpin, Vattier and Maupi—hamming it up at the Café Riche on the Canebière in our famous southern city.

Oh yes, I forgot to tell you. After all the speeches at the Académie were over, the writer Marcel Brion came toward me in his handsome green uniform and said amicably, "When are you going to join our ranks? We're expecting you, you know!"

That's a good one.

The Union des Artistes, which represents all branches of the entertainment world, has revived the annual evenings when its members put on amateur circus numbers dreamed up and organized by themselves. I had participated a number of times since the evenings were first inaugurated at the Nouveau Cirque on the Rue Saint Honoré in 1920. Looking back, I think the first act I ever presented was probably the most inspired.

Max Dearly, the great actor and my idol, played the father and Raimu and I the brother-sister acrobats. I was the son, in a pair of tights, and Raimu the daughter in a tutu and a curly blond wig, with a supposedly invisible wire attached to the back of his belt. Raimu and I did the tricks, and Max Dearly took the bows, indicating his "offspring" with a sweep of his hand.

Our act had been carefully worked out beforehand, not without many anguished groans from Raimu, who was anything but athletic. Thanks to the wire that raised him and lowered him and held him secure, we were able to accomplish some pretty convincing acrobatic tricks. First Raimu did a handstand with both his hands on mine, then with one hand and finally just a finger. The act came to a comic conclusion when Dearly and I walked away leaving Raimu suspended by his wire and howling and flailing the air.

On the night of the performance Max added an extra fillip which neither Raimu nor I expected. Coming back to take his final bow, he executed a perfect cartwheel to the accompaniment of wild laughter and applause. For a moment I felt betrayed. And then, before I knew what I was doing, I found myself making a series of some thirty cartwheels and flips around the entire ring. I returned to my starting place to find Max undone and Raimu too dumbfounded and startled to protest.

Later on I had the privilege of emceeing these occasions two or three times, I don't remember which. All I know is that I set a record which was allowed me in deference to my age. So I've seen many of these events; and

I found the 1969 version one of the best, if not the best, to date. Today's youngsters shine not only on the stage but also in the ring, on this one night a year when they risk their necks in a great show of generosity. They do it to entertain the public and also to prove that they are worthy to inherit a great tradition. Bravo, kids.

General de Gaulle's referendum has just produced some unexpectedly dramatic results. The "nos" had it, and France and the world at large were caught by surprise. Today it's May 1 and three days since the General resigned. The relative silence which greeted this gesture from our grand old man suggests the calm before the storm.

It's May 4 and the storm hasn't broken yet. There are signs of renewed violence in the *lycées,* but so far no serious outbursts. As for the General's permanent retirement, let's all touch wood. Everybody seems to feel a certain sadness tinged with respect. Up to now the reaction has been one of silent acceptance, a sort of yielding to the inevitable. The journalist Emmanuel d'Astier ended his article in this morning's *Journal de Dimanche* with the words "From Tokyo to New York, from France to Italy and Germany, the young people of this world are expressing their outrage at the state of things, at power, at war, at profits and the consumers' society, and it's time we listened to them. Let's not be a nation of old men."

Old men, eh. So much for us!

Finally my new role is fitting me better. Nothing contributes more to this happy state of affairs than the encouragement famous writers are giving me. In addition, an important Paris publisher has just asked me to compile "My Little Rules," a collection of maxims that experience has suggested to me. And there are offers from Americans as well, including a book of photographs and text about "The Paris of My Heart."

So I have a lot of things on my mind these days. I don't want to disappoint the writers and editors who have confidence in me. My new life is taking me in new directions. It was a good idea to hang up my boater.

Louise de Vilmorin, a writer and a good and faithful friend, arranged the meeting, and naturally I was proud and pleased. It's not every day that you get to meet André Malraux, the recent French Minister for Cultural Affairs and one of our greatest writers.

Like everybody else, I have always admired his literary brilliance and his learning. But I had never met him. I told Louise I was going to be nervous.

I was so nervous, in fact, that Félix and I arrived half an hour early at Lasserre's, where we were having lunch, and had to walk around the Palais de Glace twice before it was time for our rendezvous at the famous restaurant.

We waited a couple of minutes at the table reserved for us, and there he was. We leaped to our feet. He shook our hands so casually you'd have thought he was Mr. Nobody and then ordered Bloody Marys for Louise and himself. Félix and I had to order two tomato juices. We were handicapped from the start.

And you know what happened? The man I was so terrified of spent two and a half hours asking me fascinating questions about the entertainment worlds I had known since I was young! When we parted I was left with the indelible impression of a man who was familiar with every conceivable subject. And he, according to Louise de Vilmorin, was highly enthusiastic about this encounter between what he called "the last of the great Parisians."

He is as proud as I am to have been born in Paris.

What's more, he has invited me to join him in an official box at the Opéra for the May 16 gala of the Legion of Honor, at which the ballerina Ludmilla Tcherina will perform. Louise told me that we will be just the three of us in the box: herself, André Malraux and me.

I can't believe it.

We went to see Georges Wilson's production of *Arturo Ui* by Bertolt Brecht at the Théâtre National Populaire in the Palais de Chaillot. It's a very impressive show and another victory for Georges Wilson, who has had the difficult task of following in the footsteps of the famous director Jean Vilar at one of our several state-subsidized theaters. The actor Robert Hirsch, who played this kind of nightmare puppet Hitler, was brilliant from one end of the play to the other.

One remark comes to mind—again. A lot of the entertainers and actors you see these days seem to feel obliged to wear themselves out. They go into genuine fits during the course of each performance and yell so hard that you wonder if they intend to survive. Perhaps they have decided to bring the world down around their ears themselves rather than wait for history to do it. Well, there's a certain nobility in that.

Carmen Tessier and Marcel Bleustein-Blanchet asked me to accompany them to a preview showing of Jules Dassin's *Black Power*. The audience of distinguished Parisians sat breathless with admiration throughout this latest work of one of the world's great movie-makers.

The film was made in Cleveland, where the strife between blacks and whites has been particularly bloody. It's amazing that a white man could view the problem with such understanding. He shows us this festering sore which has infected the entire United States and may spread to the rest of the world. It's obvious that Jules Dassin, one of the gentlest people alive, is out to shock us into recognition of this danger, and he succeeds.

When somebody asked me afterward what I thought of the film, I answered, "It's pretty black."

Black and powerful.

Recently Carmen Tessier asked me to supper with several young people. At first I was a bit overcome by the difference in our ages despite their welcoming expressions. Then all of a sudden we clicked. A lovely, dynamic young woman said her husband had asked her to get all my books. Almost choking on my pastry, I thanked her for the encouragement and from that time on the evening was smooth sailing. She also informed me that she devoted a lot of her time to helping the children of the poor and asked me about my Ménilmontant childhood. There I was really in my element! We all got along so well that we were the last ones to leave the restaurant.

When we were just about to say goodbye, I learned that the young woman in question was the wife of Jean-Jacques Servan-Schreiber, the editor of the important weekly magazine *L'Express,* the French equivalent of *Time.* I got the biggest laugh of the evening when I turned to Félix Paquet and said, "That's that. Tomorrow morning, Félix, we take out a subscription to *L'Express.*"

I forgot to tell you. During the lunch with Malraux, Salvador Dali and his wife and a beautiful tall girl walked into the restaurant. Seeing Malraux, Dali came over to say hello. The beautiful girl came too.

We all got up for her. Amanda was her name, and Louise seemed to know her. She was really quite lovely. Then we all sat down again and André Malraux whispered in my ear, "I hate to tell you, but we just stood up for a transvestite."

"Amanda?" I said, incredulous. He nodded his head gravely. "Amanda."

Well, with my theatrical experience I should know one when I see one; but Amanda really had me fooled!

The last few months have buffeted me around so much that sometimes I've lost track of who I am and where I am. One thing is certain: Many of the distinguished people I've met have been a real help to me. Some of their courage and conviction has rubbed off on me, and they've given me reason to hope that I would eventually come to myself again. And I have. I've realized that all my efforts to make myself into a man of the world have nothing to do with my real goal, which is to leave this world in a dignified fashion. My true salvation lies in returning to my roots and staying there.

After all, the story of my life is a wonderful saga about a child of the poor. Why try to change it? I could serve as an inspiration to other children of the poor. Listen, I could tell them, don't let your inferiority complexes get you down. Choose your road and follow it confidently. What others learn in college, you'll learn from experience, the best teacher, they say! With courage, common sense and determination, you're bound to win.

I'd wave the banner of my origins. My birthright would be my finest title, my shiniest decoration.

The sun is shining in my heart and making everything seem clear. My thoughts are back in Ménilmontant and I know exactly where I am.

People don't seem to understand.

I don't want to be the pawn of glittering social groups that jostle each other for front-row center in the public eye. I'm not criticizing them; I'm in no position to. Often I've amused myself by trying to keep up, and I'm still tempted from time to time.

But that's not how I want to spend my last years. I've got to learn to say a firm but friendly no. Now that I've learned what I need and don't need for my peace of mind, it shouldn't be too hard. I know which people are good for my morale. From now on I'll attempt to stick with people and things that conform with my mentality. Not that I behaved so differently before; it's just that now these rules of thumb have begun to be indispensable. Some social sets don't consider me to be their ticket. That's all right; they're not mine either. What they want and what I want are two different things. My goals would bore them silly. We're miles apart, that's all.

The more I think about it, the more I realize how sensible I was to stop performing. If I had gone on, I certainly wouldn't have been getting any better; but what with all the help and encouragement I've been receiving, there's a chance I may make progress in my writing. It's become my most important helpmate. I've sunk my old love for the stage into my new love for writing and have discovered that I can express myself more deeply in my books than in my songs, where I was obliged to stick to the style I'd made my own. Finally I've seen the light: my goals conform with my pastime and my pastime conforms with my goals. A perfect harmony is built into my life.

A weight is off my mind. Somehow I've found the answer to the slow death of retirement. I might even become a philosopher in my old age and an inspiration to all! My fears of bogging down are gone, and I feel I have every reason to be confident.

For example—with the help of Nicole Alphand (wife of the former Ambassador to Washington) and her lovely niece, we came in first once again at one of those events where you sign your books for charity. This time the occasion was the Après-midi du Livre des Écrivains Anciens Combattants, in which all the participants are war veterans as well as authors.

Just one more of those pleasures which life has in store for me!

Up to now I've had the feeling that I was writing left-handed. From now on I'll try to do better with my right hand.

I have the great good fortune to live in a beautiful house on grounds that get prettier every day. Peace and harmony have reigned there ever since Félix and Maryse

Paquet consented to come help me live and entertain. I'm surrounded by affection on every side.

I'm lucky in other ways too. My health is giving me a respite. I've been able to go on being the man I've always been—a man of energy and good will. Meanwhile I meet more interesting people all the time, and some have become my friends. I'm evolving in a superior world where people accept me as I am: respectful, admiring, and also humbly proud of my origins.

You'll laugh, but I'm pretty choosy about the people I admire. Some people are laudable but not in ways that mean a lot to me. It's a matter of personal choice. I have to feel strongly about somebody really to admire him. And that's the way I feel about the three couples that came to lunch yesterday: the Minister Louis Joxe, Maurice Genevoix, Roland Dorgelès and their wives, and also about Madame Jean Voilier, the poet Paul Valéry's muse, a lovely example of dignity and wisdom.

It was a perfect May afternoon. The house was flooded with sun. I have every reason to believe that my guests spent two pleasant and relaxed hours with me. As is our wont, we stood at the front door for one last wave before our guests disappeared in the direction of the Parc de Saint-Cloud, which they have to cross to get back into Paris. My happiness after these lunches is all the greater now that I no longer have to worry about performing that evening!

The rest of the day went as follows: a friendly visit over tea, then some reading, then a simple family supper while watching television, bed at nine-thirty, more reading until eleven and then presto! into the land of dreams. Just like a baby, ladies and gentlemen.

I'm not telling tales. This is the true story of an old man who still has the capacity to marvel at things and who wants to hold onto it until he breathes his last. And hopes he does that smiling.

Shame, by the great Swedish movie-maker Ingmar Bergman, proves once again that you don't have to resort to fancy camera work to hold your audience's attention, when simplicity and sobriety will do the job.

Last night was the gala evening at the Opéra for the Legion of Honor. When I arrived I found André Malraux waiting for me at the bottom of the inside staircase where the official guard was already stationed. The Minister took the stairs two by two. I came puffing after him, determined not to let him out of my sight. By the time I arrived at the box, both he and Louise were there. We had a good view of the audience—everywhere you looked you saw a famous face. A lot of them were looking up at André Malraux. I assessed my man: about six feet tall, handsome, elegant, and—I can assure you, now that I know him better—unusually human and direct.

As always, I had some difficulty rising to the occasion at first. When will I learn how to breeze through these galas? When I was performing before this crowd, I had no trouble with them at all; it's only now, when I'm meeting them face to face, that I've begun to botch up our relationship. I just don't know how to set the tone.

This particular evening went perfectly well, however. Tcherina was brilliant and I was proud to be photographed with my distinguished companions. So why did I go home to La Louque disgruntled? Because I could see that old Ménilmontant was going to hang onto my coattails forever. Even my coattails made by Hawes and Curtis of London.

Certain of the older and more glorious gentlemen at the Opéra were sporting enough medals to cover the entire left side of their jackets. André Malraux wore a simple bar with four high decorations. And I . . . well, I had trotted out my very best four, and they just barely made the grade.

Day before yesterday, while we were eating supper and watching the news on television, I got a telephone call from the Paris Hilton. It was Alan King, one of the finest comedians in the land of show business, America.

If I remember correctly, he's English by birth and earned his success on the other side of the Atlantic without any fuss or fanfare. He kept going up and up until he found himself at the top with Bob Hope and other champions of a good honest laugh. Alan is tall and well built, but also elegant and graceful. And what a wit! A real ace.

Alan King. I wonder what he wants?

Hello, Alan? Are you in Paris? Yes he was, and he began to tell me in his clear and musical American English that he had just had supper with Pierre Salinger and his wife and that the talk had come around to me. Salinger confirmed my decision to leave the stage, and Alan had wanted to tell me that he, and a lot of entertainers he knew, thought I was dead right to have done it. I was very moved by his encouragement. I explained that I had wanted to step down before old age took its toll and while I was still "on top" and in high demand.

He answered, "Well, Maurice, you can just go on telling yourself that for all of us in show business and your fans in America, you'll always be on top." And then he closed with "Don't be sad, Maurice. You're great."

"Goodbye, Alan," I said, "and thanks for thinking of me."

So now you understand the transformation in my life, all of you who helped me so much when I was a performer. Don't worry, I still need your support. What's happened is simple: I've put down my boater and taken up my pen. All the heart and soul that used to go into my songs now goes into my writing. And it's all because I want to keep in touch with you, the public that I love.